Beacons Along a
Naturalist's Trail

Beacons Along a Naturalist's Trail:

California Naturalists and Innovators

Paul F. Covel

Drawings by Rex Burress

Western Interpretive Press
in association with
Western Heritage Press

Copyright © 1988 Paul F. Covel
Published by
Western Interpretive Press
2860 Delaware Street
Oakland, CA 94602
in association with
Western Heritage Press
Box 5108 Elmwood Station
Berkeley, CA 94705

Library of Congress Cataloging-in-Publication Data:

Covel, Paul F., 1908–
Beacons along a naturalist's trail.

Includes index.
1. Naturalists—California—Biography.
I. Title.
QH26.C64   1988   508'.092'2   [B]   87-34691
ISBN 0-931430-01-1

Contents

Acknowledgements   vii

Foreword *by James F. Covel*   ix

Preface *by Rex Burress*   xi

1. The Shy Scientist—Frank Stephens   1
2. Friend of Animals and Men—
   Frank Forest Gander   13
3. A Man Who Molded Generations—
   Brighton C. Cain   26
4. The Nature Lady—Amy Rinehart   39
5. Mister Parks—William Penn Mott, Jr.   52
6. Peerless Teacher, Tireless Traveler—
   Junea W. Kelly   72
7. She Saved Seashores and Sanctuaries—
   Laurel Reynolds   86
8. Botanist of Del Norte—
   Ruby Steele Van Deventer   106
9. The Naturalist's Naturalist—
   Joshua Aaron Barkin   118
10. Bird Bander of Benicia—
    Emerson Austin Stoner   133
11. Something Special—
    Elizabeth Cooper Terwilliger   143

Index   150

Maps

1. Southern San Diego County   4
2. East Bay Cities and Regional Parks   28
3. Plumas and Sierra Counties   46
4. San Francisco Bay Region   83

Photographs

Frank Stephens 2
Stephens Cabin, Mason Valley 10
Frank F. Gander at Kissing Rocks Garden 18
B. C. "Bugs" Cain with rattlesnake 32
William Penn Mott, Jr. at Children's Fairyland 57
William Penn Mott, Jr. at a new regional park 64
William Penn Mott, Jr. and Smokey 69
Junea W. Kelly 77
Laurel Reynolds with portable blind 92
Laurel Reynolds and Mindy Willis 100
Laurel Reynolds and Roger Tory Peterson 104
Ruby and Arthur Van Deventer 112
Josh Barkin and students 125
Josh Barkin makes a point 131
Emerson Stoner blows an egg 136
Emerson Stoner with Ross' Goose 141
Elizabeth Terwilliger 149

Acknowledgments

T HIS BOOK WAS actually conceived many years ago when I realized that the lives and careers of these talented, dedicated and caring men and women who interpreted their natural world and who encouraged and supported aspiring young naturalists should someday be written. When I finally began putting this together, I was aided and encouraged immeasurably by former co-workers and relatives of my subjects who generously supplied background information and took the time to review and comment on the various chapters. Completion of these biographic sketches would not have been possible without this assistance.

Special thanks are due Pearl Barkin who provided so much material on Josh Barkin; to Ariel Parkinson, daughter of Laurel Reynolds, and to Mindy Willis for the material on Laurel and Eric Reynolds; and to Marjorie Elmore, daughter of Emerson Stoner, for her help with the Stoner chapter. Each contributed generously background materials and guidance in the writing of the respective chapters. Chris Nelson and retired naturalist Dick Angel of the East Bay Regional Park District reviewed the chapter on Barkin, while Harlan Kessel, a park district director, retired General Manager Richard Trudeau, and Chris Nelson reviewed the Mott chapter. Elmer Aldrich and Morgan Harriss, early followers of "Bugs" Cain, reviewed his chapter and gave valuable input.

Rex Burress, naturalist-writer-artist of the Oakland Parks and Recreation staff, contributed the Preface, while my son James, naturalist and park and recreation professional, wrote the Foreword explaining the history of interpretation of the natural world.

My devoted wife Marion encouraged and sustained me from the start of this manuscript, acting as co-editor, censoring many an ill-chosen word or phrase, suggesting the proper approach to delicate subjects, and finally performing much of the mechanical work and corrections that brought it to completion.

I am also grateful to the following persons and institutions who contributed invaluable information, photographs and news clippings: Charmian Ariotti, Rimo Bacagelupi, Jerry Cosgrove, Flora Covell, Bill Gracie, James Crouch, August Frugé, Knowland Park Oakland Zoo, Marjorie Lessard, Richard Mewaldt, Oakland *Tribune*, Plumas County Museum, Gordon Eric Reynolds, San Diego Museum of Natural History, San Diego Zoological Society, Arthur Baller and John Michaels (ret.) of California State Parks, Ray Sutliff of the Boy Scouts of America, John Tashjian, Stephen D. Veira of the National Park Service at Arcata, and to all others who contributed to this book.

Foreword

THERE WAS A TIME in this country's not so distant past when we began to come to grips with the future of America's natural resources. The science of biology was still primitive, and specialties such as ecology and wildlife management were concepts yet to be developed. Still, a few biologists were alarmed with the rate at which our flora and fauna were vanishing and realized that an attempt must be made to describe and catalog our natural heritage while the opportunity existed. Thus an interesting new breed of adventurer appeared which was popularly referred to as a field "naturalist" or "collector."

Some of these naturalists were well educated, many were self-made students of nature. The principal objective was to go afield and collect specimens which represented the native flora and fauna of habitats throughout the country, with a particular focus on the west, where much of the plant and animal life was relatively undescribed. The ideal collector was a good shot with rifle or shotgun, an able outdoorsman who could travel in the field for months at a time, could prepare his own specimens, and was willing to live this nomadic life for little personal gain other than the satisfaction of contributing to our knowledge of our natural heritage.

As science progressed the mission of the traditional biological survey teams diminished. Some of the naturalists were relegated to museums where they continued to work with volumes of material collected by their peers. But a select few could see that a new thirst for knowledge was growing on the part of the general public. Our society was becoming increasingly urbanized and isolated from nature. Children and adults wanted to learn about the wonders of the natural environment and the ways of other creatures that share this planet with us. Into this growing information gap fell some of these field naturalists who were able to popularize the existing scientific knowledge of the day.

Thus the naturalist put down his traps and guns and picked up a camera, a pen, and became a communicator. The term "interpreter" was developed to describe someone who was able to interpret the natural or cultural environment to the public and communicate environmental principles to others. Many of us are familiar with the ranger leading a nature walk, the nature writer and his books or columns, or the work of photographers who bring nature into our living rooms. These are but a few of the efforts which are the result of the work done by naturalists, conservationists, and interpreters.

Things began to come full circle, as all things do in nature, and again these environmentalists became increasingly concerned with the rapid loss of critical resources and natural areas, just as their mentors had nearly five decades earlier. The special talents of many of these people were brought to bear in leading fights to save parklands, critical habitats, and other significant natural resources along with the various life forms dependent upon them. The life work of the conservationists and naturalists presented in these chapters is a blend of triumph and tragedy, of foresight and frustration as they fought battles to insure the future survival of those things which make our lives not only possible but also meaningful.

Paul Covel has transcended these generations of naturalists, from collector to naturalist to interpreter he has been a pioneer in this field from its inception. This collection of biographies and personal recollections represents the evolution of interpretation through the contributions of key individuals. Many of these people may not be familiar, but the results of their labors are quickly recognized and they have indeed enriched our lives.

JAMES COVEL
June 1987

Preface

Working with Paul Covel for fourteen years at Oakland, California's Rotary Natural Science Center gives me an insight into the creativity that propelled Paul to pursue and prepare this fine addition to natural history lore.

It takes a special force to both recognize the value of nature relationships to the human community and have the ability to devise a creative method of making the information useful and understandable.

What vital ingredient makes a person a naturalist and a writer? And what gives a naturalist the compulsion to write about other naturalists, researching and arranging the material at considerable time and effort? Underlying the naturalistic lifestyle is a marvelous quality perhaps not fully explainable but connected with a love of life and a desire to share joy with members of the human race. John Muir touched on this trait when he said, "I care to live only to entice others to look at nature's loveliness with understanding." That of course doesn't explain where he got the motive or how, but does indicate there is an intertwinement of early life environmental interaction and acquired knowledge.

Along Paul's life path he acquired a passion for nature, and his outgoing style and a flair for showmanship led to nature lecturing—and eventually to his being employed by the Oakland Park Department as the first municipal park naturalist in western America.

What is a naturalist? Strictly speaking, Webster says a naturalist is a person who studies nature. Doing it for pay for the public's benefit puts it in a more formal mode but the essence is the same whether it's a professional job or amateur undertaking. The larger question is why do some people become extremely interested in studying nature and devote their entire lives to the pursuit of nature study?

Paul experienced a fairly normal childhood in the suburbs of Boston, Massachusetts, where he was born in 1908, and was as intrigued with trout and tadpoles and butterflies as any active curious child. In 1923 his parents moved to San Diego, and it was there that his nature world began to expand, first with Frank Stephens, former director of the San Diego Museum of Natural History, and later with the San Diego Zoo.

Paul moved to Oakland in 1926 and went on to several nature-related jobs around the country involving museum work, collecting expeditions, botany and horticultural projects. But through it all ran a thread of devotion to interpreting the natural sciences and expounding on their virtues.

When I joined the City of Oakland naturalist staff in 1961 as animal keeper, there was already a well-established program bringing people and nature together. Paul tilted his Smokey Bear hat, scanned my qualifications, and asked me about the bird nest in a Lakeside Park oak tree. I had seen enough Missouri fox squirrel nests to know it was squirrel and not bird, and we went on from there to explore plants, animals, and minerals until Paul retired in 1975. He didn't really retire his interests, and he didn't retire as a naturalist, only as a city employee. A naturalist is forever.

Any of the people described so adeptly in this book could tell you that age and time does not diminish the zest for nature enthusiasm when the mysterious wild nature bug has bitten.

Many of these personalities put tremendous energy into the pursuit of projects and plans related to the betterment of nature. Personal effort and study and application often overshadowed formal degrees as these messengers of the out-of-doors sought to spread the gospel of natural history. Paul in particular preached conservation and became a conservation writer for several organizations. Always eager to extend a word for nature and animal life, he took time in spite of his hurried pace to stop and show a kid a snake—or a lizard—or a plant—or a bird—even a bird skin because, like so many naturalists, Paul was not reluctant to skin and stuff an animal for taxidermy mounting purposes. His practical outlook allowed hunting of needed specimens, and wildlife management control sometimes indicated a certain harvest of the surplus.

Although nature never gets old, naturalists do—and sometimes die—but the contributions they make to the storehouse of knowledge extends the richness of wildlife wonder to distant generations. Their inspirational messages go on forever.

REX BURRESS
June 1, 1987

The Shy Scientist:
Frank Stephens

A SOLITARY MAN and his burro finally came to a stop in a grove of mesquite not far from a high mesa that rose above a narrow, winding stream. Shadows were lengthening and a few cumulus clouds gathering over distant ranges somewhere in eastern Arizona promised another sunset spectacular.

The wanderer removed a bedroll from the burro, a sack of cooking paraphernalia, a sack of clanking metal traps, and then a heavy box which he handled carefully. The patient beast was hobbled and turned out to graze. The camper then set out to inspect the immediate vicinity.

Yes, there were animal tracks and diggings aplenty. Mostly they belonged to the abundant desert rodents—white-footed and pocket mice, kangaroo rats, ground squirrels, and a large burrow with signs suggesting a badger had set up residence amid this bountiful food supply. Everywhere there were footprints of coyotes

1

and even one set left by a desert white-tailed deer. Suddenly the sign-reader came upon a set of larger prints made by humans wearing moccasins! He shook his head and studied the surrounding landscape, particularly the rim of the high bluff. Then he returned to camp for his heavy set of traps and a small bag of bait.

This was young Frank Stephens, collector for the United States Biological Survey, working alone in the Apache country of eastern Arizona in the 1880s.

Stephens had seen much of the mid-west in his early youth. His parents, infected with the westward migration mania, moved from his birthplace in western New York State when he was thirteen. New lives were tried in Michigan, Illinois, Missouri, and Kansas before young Frank struck out on his own.

Romance stopped him awhile in Colorado where he met and married Elizabeth in 1874. The following year it was south to New Mexico where they settled in Indian country at Fort Bayard. Frank had acquired some reputation as a field naturalist and was gathering bird and mammal specimens for eastern museums.

Trouble broke out between the local Indians and the settlers, forcing the young couple to pull up stakes and move. Their horses

Frank Stephens.

had already been stolen but the oxen had been spared. So westward they headed with their worldly goods riding in an ox cart, California bound! But before following Frank Stephens' fascinating career on a new frontier let's return to that lone trapper in Apache country.

"I guess I slept pretty lightly that night, with my rifle nearby," Stephens told three of us boys. "Next morning after getting all the animals caught on my trapline, I took a hike up on that mesa. There they were, outlined in the tall grass right on the rim opposite my camp, three human impressions. Those Apache had been watching me all right. If I had been prospecting or shooting game they might have collected my scalp!"

The locale of this experience with Frank Stephens was his homestead in Mason Valley (originally La Puerta) on a high desert in the shadow of the pine-capped Lagunas in eastern San Diego County. The year was 1924 and this pioneer naturalist was in his late sixties.

This expedition to La Puerta marked the culmination of several collecting-campout trips made with Stephens by three teenaged aspiring naturalists of San Diego. Shorter trips to canyons north of San Diego, relatively wild spots in those days, had persuaded this old timer to take a chance on a longer safari with his three protégés. Our hunting and trapping skills were sharpening fast, and we were turning out acceptable scientific study skins for our collections. Parents of the boys had finally given permission, though I remember two took considerable convincing that unfriendly Indians and wild animals would not offer serious risks.

Getting to this part of the Colorado Desert on the old Butterfield Stage route via Descanso and Julian was an adventure in itself, but accomplished in one day if all went well. Stephens' trusty old Reo might have been capable of twenty-five miles per hour in high gear on the level, but there wasn't much level on that ninety-mile journey. Most of the way it was a crawl up and down hill in low gear that often allowed us to jump out and run ahead. The driver didn't like this demonstration—a put-down of his dependable Reo.

The acid test came in late afternoon. After traversing miles of sandy desert roads beyond Julian, we came to Box Canyon, the hidden gateway to La Puerta. Passage meant following a stream bed with ninety-degree turns and jutting banks that threatened to wipe out running boards or any exposed anatomy of passengers. We didn't dare speak to our leader, crouched over the wheel. No

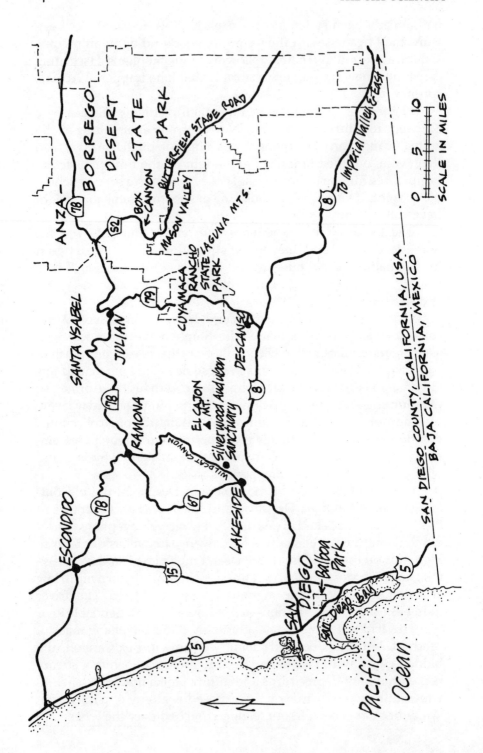

wonder that old stage route through Box Canyon long afterward became a historic landmark with modern motorists peering down from a paved highway high above it.

But the faithful Reo made it, as did the trucks and jalopies of a few ranchers and prospectors, even the Model T that we boys later drove there. We reached the Stephens claim before dusk on that unforgettable first adventure and were soon gathering firewood and helping Frank set out his animal trapline. Then we must have slept fitfully, anticipating the coyote chorus Stephens had promised we'd hear before dawn.

Who was Frank Stephens, besides being the custodian of three overeager young naturalists, their mentor, teacher in the ways of wild birds, mammals, and reptiles, a link to the days of wild Indians?

California at first didn't hold any bonanza for naturalist Stephens and his wife Elizabeth. Frank tried his hand at anything that paid wages, but they were forced to move to several locations to maintain any income. Perhaps the lure of the open trail and campfire that occurred whenever a new demand for bird and mammal specimens arrived from eastern museums was stronger than some of those humdrum jobs.

Unencumbered by any little Stephenses, the couple must have saved a grubstake for the small farm they purchased at Witch Creek in northern San Diego County in 1888. The local folk soon came to regard their farmer-naturalist so highly that they made him justice of the peace for the surrounding township.

Spouse, farm, and judicial duties were all put aside for a while when Dr. Frederick Coville of the United States Biological Survey summoned Frank Stephens to join his Death Valley Survey in 1891. Frank Stephens was proud of his part in that monumental study of the region that would later become Death Valley National Monument by President Franklin Roosevelt's declaration. It is uncertain whether Frank was made the official ornithologist or mammalogist for the party. He easily could have filled both roles.

"Those Ph.D. fellows from back east thought they were pretty good in the field," Stephens liked to recall. "One day someone questioned my identification of a raven that was a pretty long shot away. Dr. Coville overheard them and announced for all to hear: 'Whenever Frank Stephens identifies anything you can bet your boots that it is correct!' "

A challenge to launch a new career in science came from the

city of San Diego. It's possible that complacent Frank Stephens did shed a tear or two when he gave up the Witch Creek ranch and dear friends to make this move in 1898. Perhaps Elizabeth required medical attention or wanted more conveniences. She died the year following this move into the city. Stephens remarried within the year, this time to British-born Kate Brown, a biologist in her own right.

Now Frank Stephens was to win scientific recognition at home and abroad and, a few years later, help to put San Diego in the spotlight among scientists, museum and zoo circles—even among the growing number of tourists who were discovering this City of the Sun.

It was his book *California Mammals*, which appeared in 1906, that won him laurels and the admiration of North American biologists and students. Nothing like it had been attempted since 1857, and Baird's contribution to the Pacific Railroad Reports at that time hadn't even listed bats or the marine mammals. Now Frank Stephens' book gave detailed descriptions of some 263 species with measurements and a few drawings by his artist friend W. J. Fenn.

The author wrote, "The distribution of species herein given has been checked in the majority of species from personal observation." He thanked anonymously the various collectors who had contributed records from northern California where he had spent little time. But this herculean task, the compilation of *California Mammals* must have represented many years of collecting and note-taking, often under the most adverse conditions, hours of comparative studies of specimens in his own and other collections, and laborious writing in longhand. How many of his neighbors and acquaintances ever suspected this low-key plodding man would give issue to such a proud offspring?

The call of wild places came with an invitation from the University of California in 1907 to serve as collector on an Alaskan expedition. Once again Stephens put San Diego business on hold and headed for the Arctic. Bird and mammal specimens from that trip are still being studied at the Museum of Vertebrate Zoology on the Berkeley campus.

At the close of the second year of the Panama Pacific International Exposition in 1916, animal lovers of San Diego found a problem confronting them. "What would happen to the lions housed on one side of the park, the bears on another and some deer and elk elsewhere?" they were asking.

In their book *It Began with a Roar,** Dr. Harry M. Wegeforth and writer Neil Morgan relate vividly what followed. We remember snatches of accounts Stephens himself told us boys; this zoo experience was recalled with rarely expressed emotions.

"Dr. Harry" (as we zoo buffs came to call him), his physician brother Paul, and two other animal-loving doctors decided to form a San Diego Zoological Society. "We commandeered Frank Stephens of the Natural History Society," wrote Dr. Harry, "and thus our board of directors was born. . . ."

Within a few weeks the harassed board of park commissioners had granted the fledgling society some precious park land encompassing the present zoo and soon donated funds had accumulated to a level where they could build a row of temporary cages along Park Boulevard. Animal donations, ranging from local wildlife pets to a huge Kodiak bear brought by the Navy, began to pour in.

Who was qualified to take charge of this fast-growing collection? Frank Stephens. It was arranged for him to share his time with the Natural History Society.

"So, the next thing I knew I was running a zoo," Stephens would relate with a chuckle. "That Dr. Wegeforth could talk a man into anything. Qualifications? Oh, all my life I'd observed native animals in the field, then I'd collected and cared for them as museum specimens. Suppose a bear or a lion had gotten sick or something, by gosh?" For Frank, who never swore, that was a rare expletive. "I didn't relish very much this job I'd taken on."

The San Diego Zoo grew like a giant mushroom in Balboa Park. It soon required a full-time director, relieving Stephens of his task. But he must have watched its growth with some pride, as did I who had a minuscule part in the zoo operation some years afterward. It was destined to become, in the opinion of most zoophiles, the greatest zoological garden in the west, if not in all of North America. If only co-founder Stephens could see it at this writing! Attendance in 1986 exceeded three million visitors, who viewed 5,800 mammals, birds, and reptiles in displays arranged over 100 acres of Balboa Park. In addition the San Diego Zoo operates the Wild Animal Park with about 3,600 animals roaming over 1,800 acres of canyons and mesas thirty miles northeast of San Diego.

Perhaps it was the San Diego Society of Natural History, established in 1874 as the first scientific institution in southern Califor-

* Published in 1969 by the Zoological Society of San Diego in paperback.

nia, that had lured Frank Stephens to live in San Diego. He soon joined its small, enthusiastic membership, made some of his collections available to the society and added his influence to the growing drive to secure a museum.

The Panama-Pacific Exposition, occupying a prime site in beautiful Balboa Park, opened in 1915, a year after the opening of the Panama Canal. Monies had been raised for a group of magnificent exhibition halls. What a place and audience for a new natural history museum!

The society had to settle for downtown quarters in the former Hotel Cecil, but not for long. In 1917, the recently vacated Nevada building of the exposition was made available for a natural history museum. Soon a director of recognized scientific standing was needed. Frank Stephens was nominated and elected by the board in January 1920.

The new director probably accepted this prominent role at the insistence of wife Kate, an ambitious woman with great pride in Frank. The director's first official act was to appoint Kate as assistant director and curator of invertebrates at a salary one-third of his own modest stipend! The Stephenses would also occupy quarters in the new museum.

This situation couldn't last long. People pressures and administrative duties must have weighed heavily on Stephens, restricting his time for field work and research—and his grapes at La Puerta. He resigned as director the same year but continued as curator, as did Kate, for many years. When the museum outgrew its second exposition hall (the Foreign Arts building), the Great Depression was raging across the land. But a benefactor appeared in the form of Ellen Browning Scripps, who gave the greater part of the cost of a modern museum building, with public donations making up the remainder. The impressive new natural history museum opened in 1933 and Frank Stephens was there to see it.

This patient, shy scientist was further separated from the public in his later life by the curse of hearing loss. Perhaps that is one reason why he could put up with the company of three vociferous, rambunctious teenaged boys. We knew that he had helped and encouraged others earlier in his career. Most of these eager young naturalists were thrilled to help collect specimens in the still wild areas of San Diego County, and even beyond in desert reaches. Eventually these boys discovered that he might demand a little more from them than that exciting labor.

It was on our second or third expedition with Stephens to La Puerta. Our minds were probably focused on what exciting catches our trap lines would turn up and what we'd spot on those prowls with shotguns and binoculars through the creosote and mesquite or on the ridge toward Blair Valley where desert bighorn had been seen. Once we had come face to face with a coyote, but our birdshot loads merely dusted its flanks as it streaked away. For this I have ever since been grateful.

Then our leader and host reminded us that we had come on this trip to do a little extra work—in fact, that we had volunteered for the project. It seemed that Stephens, rancher Campbell over in Vallecitos, and several other distant neighbors had decided to break thrugh a new road bypassing Box Canyon. He threw some tools in the Reo.

This was a grueling task against formidable resistance in the form of deep-rooted creosote bush clumps, massive rigid *Atriplex*, and other desert shrubs—and, worse yet, cacti and agave or century plant. This last-named plant consists of fleshy leaves terminating in vicious spines and it grows in massive colonies. Many desert rodents such as the wood rat take shelter in these clumps.

We slaved away under a desert sun, three determined but not so brawny naturalists, trying to save face by demolishing a sufficient number of these unyielding natural obstacles for a few hours each day.

Slight, wiry Frank Stephens worked like a Trojan, matching the speed of the young rancher Campbell and a couple of other tough desert-rat types.

An exclamation of pain interrupted this work party one morning. It seemed to come from Stephens. We all looked for Frank, who had been tugging out some smaller shrubs after chopping at their roots.

There he lay, or half-sat, right in the heart of one of those bristling clusters of century plant! A stubborn root had given way easier than expected. He looked as much embarrassed as pained. Those of us first to reach him planted our feet gingerly around the spiny clusters and gradually hauled him back on his feet.

"Gosh darn it!" exclaimed Stephens. We half expected to see blood oozing through his trousers and shirt, but the spines hadn't got far within his tough hide. He refused to allow an inspection for puncture wounds, picked up his grubhoe, and returned to work.

We wish we had a record of Stephens' first words when res-

Author at Stephens Cabin, Mason Valley, c. 1955.

cued by neighbor Campbell after a fall had resulted in several days
at the bottom of the well shaft on the Stephens claim a few years
before that. This well, a product of several years of grueling, personal labor, eventually yielded a meager water supply for
Stephens' struggling vineyard.

The little vineyard served two main functions: it provided
Stephens a valid excuse when he wanted to escape from the city
and social obligations (over Kate's vehement protests), and it provided green shoots to hungry rabbits and fruit to a few birds and
foraging coyotes.

Eventually we three musketeers, Sam, Jack, and I, earned the
confidence of our teacher and idol and were given the key to the
cabin at La Puerta. This was a time when Stephens couldn't leave
San Diego and we would go on our own, after repeated requests. I
owned a Model T and would risk it on an expedition.

The Model T did finally make it through Box Canyon but not
without tight moments and many admonitions from cautious Sam.
Upon reaching the cabin there was still enough daylight left to set
out our rodent traps baited with chewed oats. Two of us were
making our own study skin collections.

Early the next day we scoured the surrounding terrain, shotguns at the ready. Our trap line catch was safely stashed back in the cabin awaiting preparation later when the afternoon sun drove most desert dwellers to seek shade.

Suddenly a long sought prize, a roadrunner, flew out of a cholla cactus clump, landed and ran off through the creosote. We had previously seen this bird near the cabin and guessed it wouldn't go far, so we fanned out in a wide circle. Sure enough, it ran out into a clearing and became the trophy of that day's collections, claimed by this mighty hunter. But how many times I regretted that lucky shot.

Back in San Diego we proudly showed off our collections to Frank Stephens. When we laid out the carefully made and labeled birdskins he uttered a little cry of dismay—our prized chaparral cock or roadrunner had long been the wild pet of Stephens' ranch, an avian character scrupulously spared whenever the owner did any hunting nearby.

If this remorseful slayer has since derived any satisfaction from converting that hapless bird and a few hundred birds and mammals in subsequent years into scientific specimens it is this: many of these specimens have been used to introduce native birds and mammals to some thousands of adult and young students. The resulting interest and knowledge has doubtless saved a greater number of animal lives. They were taken before the era of modern cameras and color photography. The Stephens roadrunner today occupies an honored niche among the birdskins used in teaching at Merritt Community College in Oakland.

Frank Stephens was struck and killed by a street car in front of his San Diego home in October 1937. A modern hearing device might have saved his life. We wonder how many more years he would have managed to make the round trip to La Puerta to take care of the grapes. By that time the roads were improved, but his driving had become so menacing to himself and others that Mrs. Stephens insisted he take along a younger companion. Kate Stephens, incidentally, lived to reach 103, and spent many more years in her study and classification of shells at their old home.

Stephens would probably not have considered himself an interpreter as the term is used today in outdoor natural science education. Nevertheless, besides writing the invaluable book *California Mammals*, the first in its field, he helped to launch two California institutions which gained renown as leading interpreters of the natural world—the San Diego Zoo and the Museum of Natural History. The real extent of his contributions in aiding and encouraging future naturalists and scientists in their youth has never been measured.

Although we did know several others who profited by their early association with naturalist Stephens, I shall report on two of the three boys mentioned. Impetuous, restless Jack settled down in college to earn higher degrees, became a biology professor at a Southern California college, a noted mammalogist, parachuted from a bomber behind enemy lines in World War II, and finally retired to an Arizona mountain retreat where he established a Frank Stephens Memorial Research Station.

Sam, the quiet introvert, served some years at both the Natural History Museum and the San Diego Zoo, helped build planes during World War II, then joined the gardener staff at Balboa Park because of his passion for plants.

The Stephens experience was an invaluable part of my formative years. The unswerving integrity and modesty of this humble scientist left its indelible stamp on us—his protégés.

It was a thrill for me to take two sons, one who would become a professional naturalist-interpreter, down through that section of Anza-Borrego State Park to view the Stephens cabin and the monument erected to him. Today the cabin is gone, but the monument stands on private land in Mason Valley. Kate Stephens chose as an inscription the following lines from Longfellow's "Fiftieth Birthday of Aggasiz":

FRANK STEPHENS 1849–1937

And Nature the dear old nurse
    sang to him night and day,
Saying here is a story book
    thy Father has written for thee.
Come wander with me, she said
    and read what is still unread.
And he wandered—away and away
    and ever the way seemed long
And his heart began to fail
    She would sing a more wonderful song
And tell a more wonderful tale.

Friend of Animals and Men:
Frank Forest Gander

Stop Yanqui! No se puedan pasar por aqui." A heavyset Mexican wearing a large sombrero and packing a very large revolver on his belt emerged from the adobe close to the flimsy gate. One of the intruders had already stepped down from the truck cab and walked toward this barricade.

"Ah Señor, estamos amigos—un expedición del Museo de San Diego. Vamos a las montañas para coleccionar animales," shouted the older of the three *norteamericanos*.

This didn't seem to satisfy or soften the big man with the pistol who strode up to the truck packed high with camping gear and paraphernalia. Now two other male figures appeared from the adobe, one packing a sidearm and the other carrying an old double-barrel shotgun.

The outlook for the three adventurous naturalists was not bright. It had been many hours since they had left a surfaced road below Jacumba on the California border to follow tortuous, sandy, or rough roads toward their objective, the towering Sierra Juarez. They knew too well that some Yankee big game hunters and prospectors had never returned from back roads like this or, if lucky, had been found days later, parched and half-starved, stripped to their underwear.

Now the three Mexicans had found the collectors' shotguns. The fact that one was a small bore and its loads birdshot didn't seem to change the situation. The older naturalist in charge of the party produced a worn briefcase and found their permits for firearms and for collecting "scientific specimens." These didn't impress the Mexicans, whose reading abilities were perhaps limited, and who hadn't yet identified themselves as *policia* or *aduana* (customs).

The third naturalist, a younger blond fellow with penetrating blue eyes and a disarming smile, whispered to his leader. Up to now he had remained an interested bystander.

"Buenos días, Señor," he greeted *El Numero Uno* with outstretched hand. "No estamos interesados en sus recursos minerales y sabemos—no tirar al ganado. El Señor Gobernador del Territorio sabe y aprovecha de nuestra expedición." This was Frank Gander, instant friend of people and animals.

A grin transformed the big Mexican as he shook the proffered hand. This assurance in just the right tones that they didn't seek minerals, wouldn't shoot a cow, and came under the governor's protection changed everything. Both of the armed backup paisanos made haste to open the gate and lifted their hats as the naturalists passed. Hey, wouldn't the señores stop in for a tequila? No, gracias, the day was waning and they must find a camp before dark.

Frank and his companions were seasoned "Baja hands." All spoke Spanish, but it may have been the "body language" that made the difference.

I made my acquaintance with Frank Forest Gander at an important phase in Gander's life and at a very crucial time in my budding career. So much of my time had been spent in following, questioning, and delaying various keepers at the fast-growing San Diego Zoo that the zoo director finally hired me as a flunky and handyman for after-school and weekend hours. It was almost too good to be true—a job in paradise.

The average zoo keeper in the mid-1920s was a rough-hewn male with little formal education but great dedication and savvy where his animals were concerned. Constant bombardment by questions from the passing public and frequent misbehavior by visitors helped toughen their hides and their responses. Many bore scars of encounters with their charges. A broom or rake handle offered a handy tranquilizer for boisterous animals like baboons and monkeys.

Frank was a mild soft-spoken keeper of slight stature who actually volunteered to take over these primates after he had tried various jobs with the zoo inhabitants. He must have seen the real possibilities behind those grimacing, teeth-grinding, shrieking, problem animals.

What followed with these belligerent baboons and sneaky, snapping spider monkeys, no one could really explain. Instead of brandishing defensive weapons, Frank just talked to them. Not only did he have to win their trust, but he had to turn off the constant ear-splitting family fights among them, at least before entering the cages. Within months this new keeper could pose with a pyramid of spider monkeys built around him!

This romance with such high-strung, temperamental creatures unfortunately could not endure forever. Other keepers secretly resented Gander's phenomenal success with the primates and with the most surly of vexing patrons.

A newly arrived female Chacma baboon, fearful and defensive, turned to Frank for protection. In fact, it looked like love at first sight. One day the zoo director stopped by as the two friends were exchanging caresses. Motivated by bravado or professional jealousy, he insisted that Frank admit him to Chacma's cage for an introduction. With some reluctance and words of caution, Frank admitted the director. Almost immediately Chacma sprung upon him and inflicted a nasty bite. He was hastily ushered out of the cage to seek first aid treatment. His remarks are not recorded.

There were other minor incidents and differences of policy and procedure between Gander and the head office. Although Frank could cope with frightened, belligerent animals, he just couldn't take arbitrary rules and excessive supervision, so he gave up his zoo job.

Frank Forest Gander first saw the light on a spring day in Kansas in 1899. As soon as he could follow an older brother into the fields and woods around Wichita he accumulated a backyard menagerie that drew attention from the local press. A family move to Florida fourteen years later revealed a very different nature scene; Frank now spent all his spare time observing and discovering.

One could guess what the United States Army did with Frank when he enlisted in World War I. They put him in the Pigeon Corps, where he showed such talents that he was promoted to sergeant. So adept was he at training new recruits in this valuable communications service that they refused to ship him overseas.

The urge to go west would soon shape Frank's life, as it has so many American naturalists of past generations. He would do it like some of those whose writings had inspired him—hiking cross country.

In the year 1920 it wasn't practical to carry a rifle and shoot your meals en route. When meager cash ran out, Frank found odd jobs to buy food. This way he reached his older sister in Wichita who encouraged him to submit some of the nature articles he had been writing. Bonanza! The editors of the *Christian Science Monitor* bought several.

Once again headed for the far west, Frank hitchhiked into Oklahoma, where he hopped a freight train that got him to Melrose, New Mexico. Here he became a ranch hand and saved enough money to return to his family in Florida for Thanksgiving, his real goal still three thousand miles away.

There must have been an easier way of reaching those golden shores of California which he envisioned as a naturalist's paradise. Next time Frank signed on as crew on a ship going west from Mobile, Alabama. Finally, in the year 1922 he reached his goal, even if it was on the beach at San Pedro.

What supported Frank as he delved into the life of the tidepools and the fauna and flora of that coast isn't recorded. Perhaps he lived off the land with the help of some friendly fishermen. He must have written more nature stories inspired by his new discoveries. Then one day he agreed to help a crippled news vendor move to San Diego. This act of kindness led to a career that was to touch and inspire thousands of southern Californians, young and old.

In 1923 Frank became a keeper at the San Diego Zoo, where we left him a while back. Romance caught up with him in the person of Mary, a frequent visitor at the zoo that summer. They were married that fall and moved into a house on the zoo grounds. Frank continued to write nature articles and was invited to give radio programs. The new Mrs. Gander quickly adapted to the interruptions, joys, and conflicts of being a naturalist's spouse.

When Frank reluctantly resigned from the zoo position in 1926 for the reasons already cited, another opening was offered just outside the zoo fence. This was the post of instructor at the O'Rourke Zoological Institute. He jumped at the opportunity; this was his best field, he'd decided.

This institute was the brain child of a Dr. Raymenton, retired psychiatrist from Massachusetts, a man of considerable charm, persuasion, and imagination who had persuaded the O'Rourke family to finance him, and the city to grant use of a vacant 1915 Exposition building.

Frank readily accepted a day and night, six- or seven-day per week schedule of slide talks and animal displays all over San Diego County. The Boy Scouts and other organizations clamored for his services. Dr. Raymenton, a demanding taskmaster, was delighted, but the salary was meager and often there wasn't money for auto expenses. The Ganders had rent to pay, and a family was in sight.

Somehow the Ganders survived this period in his career, demonstrating the talents of his bride Mary as a domestic manager. Before the end of the 1920s came the big break. "We want you to join our staff and develop a county-wide program for the schools," said the proposal from the San Diego Museum of Natural History.

Frank immediately accepted this offer. The good Dr. Raymenton was bereft of his star performer. His somewhat premature and under-funded institute didn't survive too long after that.

There remained one hurdle in Frank's future progress with the museum and the county schools—lack of a college degree. This problem he promptly tackled by registering at San Diego State College to work for his A.B. degree.

The Natural History Museum, under the leadership of a distinguished director, Clinton Abbott, and curators such as Laurence Huey and Charles Harbison, was now making waves in juvenile nature education that could be envied and imitated by science museums elsewhere. Frank found time to join Huey and Harbison, often assisted by younger naturalists like Sam Harter and Jack VonBlocker, on collecting trips across San Diego and adjacent counties and into Baja California.

During the great depression of 1929–1933, institutions suddenly lost wealthy contributors. The Natural History Museum could no longer afford to pay Frank's salary and allow him to attend college

Frank F. Gander at Kissing Rocks Garden (Marilyn Jenkins photo).

part time. It looked bad for Frank, but not for long. Benefactor Ellen Scripps, who had already promised a new museum, couldn't see it functioning without this brilliant educator. She covered Frank's salary so he could continue both at the museum and college.

After his graduation Frank put on another hat—he became supervisor of nature study for the county schools in addition to remaining on the museum staff. With President Roosevelt's crash work programs, the Works Progress Administration (WPA) and Public Works Administration (PWA), many good projects and people emerged. Such a person was Mrs. Higgins, engaged as a helper in the botany department of the museum, who helped curator Gander arrange field collections of San Diego County plants. So expert did she become that she later joined the staff and stayed on long after Gander left.

World War II, unlike the great depression, brought a setback—albeit temporary—to the museum. It was claimed as an annex to the San Diego Naval Hospital. Exhibits were hurriedly moved to storage, holes drilled everywhere for a maze of plumbing, partitions thrown up—in short, complete disruption. Frank could have continued classroom teaching, but it was too confining for his restless temperament. He wound up building aircraft like so many San Diegans.

Our association with Frank was renewed after the war when he was operating a thriving plant nursery at Lakeside, a foothill town east of San Diego. He greeted us cordially as always, but customers kept interfering with our conversation. Frank looked a bit weary and harassed by these conflicting demands of business and friendship. "This business is just too much for a man's peace of mind," he remarked as we said goodbye.

"Mr. Frank Gander has moved his nursery business from Lakeside to Kissing Rocks Garden close to Escondido and will specialize in native California plants," read a notice received a couple of years after that. In an accompanying note Frank explained that he had moved to escape the growing demands on him at the Lakeside location. Here in the hills several miles from Escondido devoted customers would still find him, and his new offerings of native materials would attract quite a few others.

The next spring a Kissing Rocks Garden visit was a must. No bothersome customers were around; we could enjoy conversation unlimited, interrupted only by the songs of mockingbirds, wren tits, song sparrows, and other neighbors. He showed the little dripping pipe and shallow basin where these birds came daily to drink and bathe and often to be caught on film.

Frank asked, "Is there still film in your camera?" When I assured him there was, he told us to sit beside him on a bench while he reached for a can of meal worms, deposited one on his knee, and began to produce squeaky sounds. Our host kept squeaking, but no bird appeared. Imagine our surprise when a blue-bellied or fence lizard suddenly materialized and seized the snack. Frank gestured toward another waiting on the path nearby and got down another worm for a similar performance. Now another achievement—that of lizard caller—had to be added to the many talents of this amazing naturalist.

Kissing Rocks Garden seemed the ideal place for Frank and Mary Gander. There were seldom too many buyers to interfere with his preferred pursuits. He began to accumulate a splendid series of pictures of the local and the migrant birds attracted by his food and water offerings. When word of this got around, friends and acquaintances began begging Frank to market his slides. This he consented to do, chiefly because he couldn't refuse, and he printed a list for their convenience. Many bird talks from that time on were enhanced by a number of the Kissing Rocks residents and visitors. Schools and colleges heard of this source of intimate bird poses and sent in orders. Now this business threatened to grow too large; Mary was kept busy packaging and mailing out slides and cashing checks. But it led her spouse to make another major move.

Perhaps it was the success or the routine chores essential to maintaining a nursery, even in this ideal setting, that again threatened Frank's peace of mind. He needed more isolation, a place to think and to write. Enough of the business world. He sold Kissing Rocks.

Big Boulder Ranch, on the edge of El Cajon Mountain, a little farther inland than Lakeside (a growing San Diego suburb), seemed like just the spot. Oh, it would take Mary a little longer to reach the stores and the road might even wash out in winter rains, but she cheerfully accepted another move.

It was here in the mid-1960s that Frank was to achieve adventures in man-wildlife relations that gained him wide attention in the local media, a feature article in the June 1965 issue of *Pacific Discovery,* and stories in other magazines. After all, he did love to write and to see his wild neighbors in print. It's doubtful that he and Mary were ever prepared for the wave of letters and phone calls from people seeking to visit that invariably followed such stories.

A most shy and elusive little mammal is the *Bassariscus* or ring-tailed cat (no cat at all, but a cousin of the raccoon) that ranges across the southwest and through the foothills and lower mountains up into northern California. It is rarely seen nowadays by nature seekers and campers, even though the 49ers persuaded it to live around their cabins to keep the rats and mice under control. An equally elusive mammal is the spotted skunk, a slightly smaller creature that lacks the boldness often displayed by the common skunk. It shares a range very similar to the *Bassariscus* but may accept more civilization than the former.

Both these mammals occur in the western foothills of San Diego County wherever adequate wild habitat exists. It didn't take long for them to find the grapes put out for them in the dry season, and only a little longer to discover their benefactor.

Frank would disappear shortly after dusk on many evenings from spring to fall and make his way to his bait station in a secluded canyon site. As darkness fell the spotted skunks first appeared. A ring-tail would appear shortly afterward. As the weeks passed each species grew bolder. The outcome was inevitable; both ring-tails (a second one had joined the party) and spotted skunks sat up on Frank's knees, taking tidbits from his hands! They preferred to approach separately, but in moments of greed or jealousy, both species might briefly share his lap. Other wild neighbors lured by Frank's offerings and reassuring manner included wood rats and gray foxes, one prey and the other predator, who somehow avoided encounters.

The soft bark emitted by the *Bassariscus* when excited confirmed what Frank had long suspected. There had been ring-tails in the vicinity of Kissing Rocks Garden and around several campsites he had occupied in San Diego County. But a more intimate revelation was in store for our nature man.

As Frank studied the ring-tails mouthing tidbits and romping back and forth in early May, he realized from the condition of the female's teats that she must be nursing. The whereabouts of the offspring remained a great mystery for many weeks. Then one evening in late July the proud mother brought in her litter, four very agile and spirited youngsters. Gander's cup overflowed.

Before my wife and I could get around to visiting our friend's lair at Big Boulder Ranch another surprise announcement arrived in the mail in August 1966. Frank Gander had become resident naturalist at Silverwood Audubon Sanctuary. This lovely quiet place, nestled among oaks, boulders, and chapparal a few miles east of Lakeside on the Wildcat Canyon Road, is owned and managed by the San Diego Audubon Society. The urgent invitation to accept this challenge had enticed the Ganders from their mountain retreat.

The next spring we headed for Silverwood* accompanied by our buddy Sam and his wife Jane from San Diego. Wildcat Canyon in spring is a thrill for any nature lover. The sweet scents of chaparral pervade the roadside, coming from an association of chamise, toyon, hollyleaf cherry, mountain lilac (*Ceanothus* sp.), sagebrush and other shrubs. Clumps of dark green live oak and light, flamboyant sycamores mark the little watercourse, while bright orange splotches of dodder are splashed over the chaparral.

The short path from the Silverwood parking lot up to headquarters runs through a tunnel of ceanothus. Bird songs and calls echoed all the way.

Frank was waiting outside the combined residence and office-visitor reception. He called out to Mary, who greeted us and then vanished; she had always insisted that her spouse occupy the center of attention.

Suddenly something moving very fast appeared close to our faces, shifting from us to Frank and back. A bumblebee was our first thought. But no, it wore feathers. Just as suddenly it came to rest on Frank's outstretched hand. It was a beautiful male Anna hummingbird.

"Don't mind Bozo," said our host softly, "he isn't content with filling himself at the feeding station but wants to inspect everyone who comes on the place. He's startled quite a few visitors; don't know what we're going to do about him!"

Many more hummers darted past or paused to taste the variety of flowers, mostly chaparral species such as red monkey flower, white sage, and climbing penstemon that highlight the trail up to the big rocks on the hillside. Some herbacious flowers brighten small clearings such as *Mimulus Fremontii* and the stately *Penstemon spectabilis*. As mid-day drew near most bird voices were stilled except for ever-exuberant species such as the wrentit and Bewick's

---

* Silverwood Audubon Sanctuary is normally open to visitors on Sundays from 9 to 4. The address is 13003 Wildcat Canyon Road, Lakeside, CA 92040. Further information may be obtained from the San Diego Audubon Society at 2270 Fifth Avenue, San Diego, CA 92101.

wren, scolding scrub jays, and occasional quail calling together or warning their broods.

Frank produced some large scrapbooks filled with black and white photos of his animal neighbors. These included the mammals that ordinary visitors never glimpsed by day. Frank had developed a night rendezvous and feeding station a little way up the canyon at Silverwood. Here were more ring-tails, spotted skunks, raccoons, foxes, and wood rats, all responding to call and some hand tame.

No piece of paradise or Garden of Eden is safe in today's world, no matter how miniscule and remote. Frank was embroiled in a sharp controversy with the powerful county health and vector control services. San Diego County had made headlines for the number of rabid skunks found that year. The ensuing poisoning operation inevitably had destroyed many of the other small carnivores that shared skunk habitat.

County trappers and poisoners were operating on neighboring ranchland all around Silverwood. Only one skunk had responded to Gander's handouts that spring, and gray foxes and raccoons had decreased to a handful. While the sanctuary of Silverwood might be respected, any of its animal inhabitants who ventured outside the boundaries were in dire peril.

Frank now had to patrol his borders for overzealous animal control teams. He had enlisted the help of the Audubon members and had taken his plea for moderation to the highest authorities. Entire predatory mammal populations could be lost in such an all-out campaign. After all, very few humans would come in contact with rabid wild animals, he reasoned.

It was now nature walk time. A dozen or so adult visitors and several children gathered. Some had previous experience with the Silverwood nature man and their example helped to keep the group orderly and quiet as we started out. Frank gently admonished a couple of youngsters who wanted to forge ahead.

We had barely emerged from the oaks and entered the chaparral when Frank stopped the group and gave the hush sign. "If we stay together and keep very quiet, we may see my token rattlesnake on this rock ledge we're approaching." I could see faces tense and hear hoarse whispers among three first-time visitors.

Our guide had come opposite the ledge and was speaking softly. "There it is, friends, a beautiful spectacled rattlesnake coiled up just within the shade. He may have been sunning but moved when he detected our approach. He's relatively tame, but not for stroking. He'd probably never strike unless he felt threatened."

"Buzzy" moved farther back under the rock as our column passed. He would remain the high point of many exciting experiences and introductions that afternoon. A family of young ground squirrels just out of the den were offered some sunflower seeds. Frank's vocal imitations brought a pair of wrentits in among us, and a busy anthill held the group's attention while he discoursed on the complexities of this insect society.

It was a rare treat to follow naturalist Frank on an interpretive walk. Fortunate indeed were the several volunteer nature guides who had been accepted to help Frank in educational work. Among these was Sam, who had come out of retirement because of his loyalty to Frank. Sam had shared collecting trips and campouts with Gander, and I deeply envied him these experiences.

Someone mentioned opossums as we stood around recalling past anecdotes after the walk. By this time this little introduced southerner had long since saturated the county and most of California. Frank asked, "Remember that trip when you, Sam, Jack, and I were all helping Frank Stephens back in 1926? We trapped the first opossum recorded in San Diego County. After getting the skin off we cooked it and ate it; tasted good, too!"

We revisited Frank and Silverwood two or three times after that, but not each spring as we had promised ourselves. Then one day early in 1976 a phone call from Sam delivered sad news. The nature man of Silverwood had died peacefully at his home after conducting a nature walk.

In searching for a fitting closing to Frank Gander I came upon a sheet of his poetry. Perhaps it was written from his temporary retirement home on the mountain at Big Boulder Ranch, or during a quiet day at Silverwood.

To Life

To be alive is in itself a thrill,
A thrill I share with other living things,
The many varied forms from nature's mill;
The oneness of them all a message brings.
The protoplasmic gel within the cell,
Alike in all but varying in grade,
From man to lowly worm and plants as well.
For man is part—he does not stand apart—
One species in this teeming world of life,
So in himself he finds some traits of all
And of this life man feels himself the heart,
The dominating force that leads the strife
And onward surges 'til the shadows fall.

To Death

When death arrives, cremated I would be
And have my ashes spread upon the earth,
As this would free all elements in me
For use again by life—a true re-birth.
So let my moisture rise into the sky
And join the clouds that speed the singing rills
To quicken life in regions parched and dry,
Or drop their rain upon a thousand hills.
My atoms all came to me from the past,
And all unto the future will belong.
I want no grave nor marker at my head,
Forget the man, all things worthwhile will last,
Some deeds, and writings, and perhaps a song.
The rose will bloom, 'though this one man be dead.

A Man Who Molded
Generations:
Brighton C. Cain

IT HAPPENED ON the campus of Mills College in Oakland one beautiful spring morning. The quarry had been pinned down in a patch of shrubbery. The eager pursuers were about to surround its hideout when the tall young man in khaki, with binoculars held at the ready, gave the command to freeze. Six scouts, also armed with binoculars, came to a dead halt and stopped their excited chatter.

From their leader issued a strange series of squeaks, chirps, and tut-tut-tut-tuts in rapid succession. A pause, and similar sounds came from the shrubbery. This performance was repeated several times. Finger to lips, the leader gathered his scouts around him.

"I think it may be a yellow-breasted chat, a rare transient hereabouts," he confided sotto voce. "Chats behave like that. Let's spread out around it quietly—maybe we can catch sight of the fellow."

The challenging sounds continued. Scouts and an adult male guest on the hike silently crept around the thicket. There crouched the quarry—two lovely Mills girls, both with binoculars and one

26

with an Audubon bird caller in hand. Standing aghast were six disappointed boy birders, a much embarrassed leader and a rather pleased guest birder.

Who was this leader whose fame in identifying and talking back to the birds was legendary, but who won many more laurels for his accomplishments with Boy Scouts?

It was Brighton C. Cain. By the time of the preceding incident he was known as "Bugs" Cain, a Stanford graduate in entomology who took a summer job in 1925 at Oakland's Dimond Camp of the Boy Scouts. This young counselor—who could persuade city boys to accept snakes and insects, study the way of a bee with a flower, thoughtfully finger a rock and watch wild birds and game without wanting to grab or scare—was an instant success at camp. Head scouter Homer Bemiss and the council invited him to join the permanent staff and he accepted. This was his niche. Field entomology could wait. So could romance, marriage, and anything else that might conflict with service to his boys.

The mecca of Boy Scouts in Oakland was Dimond Camp* in the lower Oakland hills. Alluring trails led off through nearby Joaquin Miller Park and through the Skyline Redwoods into the urban wilderness of the new East Bay Regional Parks. But the first goal of most of the scouts who hiked up to Dimond Camp was the Bug House—the small, unpretentious structure turned over to Bugs Cain. Signs reminded them to approach quietly; birds were being fed and caught for banding in the rear of the place. Deer, skunks, and raccoon might be seen in early morning or toward evening around Dimond Camp, though Bugs didn't welcome them to his bird feeding and banding station.

This house of wonders, the Bug House, combined elements of museum, mini-zoo, classroom, planetarium, and window lookout on the feeding station. No boy ever emerged the same as when he entered. Even the occasional sophisticated, blasé father who dutifully brought his scout would be caught in the contagion of excited boys and emerge a somewhat better man.

Most exciting of all exhibits to the visitor were the snakes. They lived mostly comfortable existences in captivity, sharing meals of mice, frogs, or lizards, according to each species' tastes. I use the term "mostly comfortable" because they were required to submit to

* Mike Dimond was an early settler (in the late 1800s) who lived at the head of the present Fruitvale Avenue on Sausal Creek.

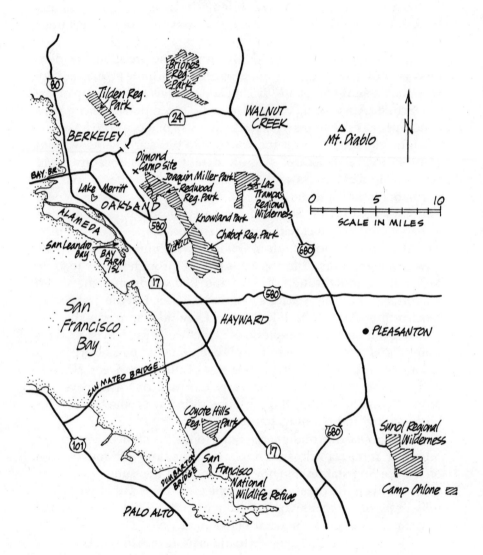

gentle, supervised handling and to accompany Bugs to demonstra-
tions at schools, clubs, summer camps, etc. Bugs' snake teachings
probably saved the lives of thousands of snakes encountered in the
wild. Only the rattlesnake cage bore a padlock. But that didn't
mean they were untouchable. Their master regularly brought them
forth, demonstrated their amiability, even took them along on his
presentations. He was able to prove a little-known scientific fact,
later confirmed by the renowned Dr. Raymond Ditmars, that a
rattler can stand only about twenty minutes of direct sunlight on its
head before fatal consequences ensue. Once he proved that a pet
rattler can't always be trusted—but that story will come later.

Merit badges for advancement were numerous and tough in
those earlier years of scouting. One of Bugs Cain's principal tasks
was to prepare and to pass applicants for a formidable array of
badges in the natural sciences and outdoor skills. Among these the
Bird Study merit badge seemed to be the toughest and even the
most dreaded by many scouts. Whenever the name of Bugs comes
up in the reminiscences of some successful business and professional men, they still recall their struggles to pass the Bird Study
merit badge.

Birding with Bugs Cain was not just a matter of learning to
identify a required number of species, their songs and calls. That
was just the beginning. Before the eager scouts could board the
venerable scout bus for the birding location, there was the "ritual of
the binoculars." This precious loaned collection had been gathered
from generous dealers and other friends of scouting. Like the tough
drill sergeant presenting the rookie with his first rifle, Bugs would
carefully clean each lens and explain the focusing controls as he
handed them out to the neophyte birders.

Once in the field it wasn't enough for Bugs' students just to
decide the proper name for the bird in the glass. Why was the bird
in that particular kind of tree or bush? What sort of insect, seed, or
fruit was it seeking? How was it using its bill or feet to secure the
food? So each boy received a mini-lesson in ecology, even if there
wasn't a merit badge for that subject at that time.

Back at the Bug House, their heads buzzing with impressions
of sightings and confusing voices, the bird badge seekers were not
finished for the day. Bugs would seat them and bring out his
collection of shoe boxes full of study skins of birds. Then would
begin a "tools of the trade" recognition quiz. Covering most of the
bird's body with his hands, he would expose a bill or foot for
identification. Scouts who had looked and listened attentively dur-

ing the field trip would pick out the swollen bill of a grosbeak, the long scratching claws of a towhee, or the flat, broad, bug-scoop bill of a flycatcher or swallow. All this they had better remember when final tests came!

Although twenty years later most of these bird badge winners couldn't have distinguished a titmouse from a bushtit, there were shining exceptions. Bugs was particularly proud of a handful of young high school birders who had organized the Oakland Ornithological Club. These dedicated youths had prepared and published a first-ever publicly available *List of the Birds of Lake Merritt and Lakeside Park.* It included 138 species.

Cain spent much time with this club and other scouts at Lakeside and other urban parks. He was enthusiastic about the parks' wealth of plant materials and wanted identification lists prepared. Conspicuous in his scout uniform and broad-brimmed hat, he became a genial question-answer man for the curious public. At other times he assumed the warden role when he caught boys with air rifles or starting fires in the hill parks. Finally the superintendent of parks and the park commissioners recognized this man's value. He was summoned to a commission meeting and handed a metal badge bearing the words: "Naturalist, Oakland Park Department." No salary accompanied this exalted title, but Bugs was immensely pleased.

And what became of the very special group of Bugs' followers, the Oakland Ornithological Club? Such juvenile organizations are generally not long-lived; the demands of higher education scatter and preoccupy them, followed by romances, careers, and marriage. Indeed, such a succession of events befell most of these young bird watchers. They became professors, farmers, government workers, naturalists, and businessmen. But the magic of Bugs' enthusiasm and leadership stayed with them. Even to the time of this writing they hold regular annual get-togethers in some natural environment and recall those rich adventures in hills and canyons, at shorelines and marshes around San Francisco Bay.

A special event staged by naturalist Cain during summer or early fall was the Indian Foods Cookout. Teaching survival skills which might someday prove useful to Boy Scouts on wilderness treks was one objective. Some things about snaring and trapping rabbits, squirrels, wild mice and gophers may have been included, or how to fashion fishhooks from pins or old bones, but how to use wild plants constituted the main theme.

Wild berries abounded in the Oakland hills, and still do: huckleberries, elderberries, blackberries (native and introduced), and a myriad of grass seeds can be harvested and ground. But more basic, filling items were needed, so Bugs dispatched trusted scouts to collect certain "nuts" or fruits (a fruit, botanically speaking, is the plant product that contains the seeds).

On Indian Foods Cookout day at Dimond Camp, Bugs supervised a number of scouts in preparations, with a handful of dads and moms usually present, motivated by curiosity or perhaps by the thought that Junior might have to be rushed to the hospital for stomach pumping later on.

Hot coals were produced by several scouts who had earlier dug fire pits and brought in firewood. There were berries in Indian baskets for preliminary snacks, and some made into a berry punch. Small piles of acorns from the local live oaks and green-brown bay nuts from the California bay or laurel were displayed, but even the grown-up observers knew you couldn't eat them raw. What they didn't know was that the master woodsman and a few assistants for the past two or three days had ground both acorns and bay nuts and placed them on fiber mats under running water to leach out bitter acids.

Then these Indian cooks ceremoniously entered the scene and placed these preparations into boiling water over the coals. One or two patient scouts even followed the Indian custom of cooking the mixtures in waterproof baskets with water kept boiling by hot rocks.

Finally came the proud time to serve the guests. Some ground seeds and berries were added to acorn bread patties and soon scouts and some daring parents ate the main dish enjoyed by many generation of the local Ohlone Indians. The bay nuts were sampled but never liked so well. Gathering of the hazelnut or wild filberts were usually meager.

In those days finding and preparing survival foods was an art practiced mostly by Boy Scouts, certain military personnel and other people planning wilderness adventures. Today one could accumulate a bookshelf on the subject. Naturalist programs and outdoor clubs schedule wild foods banquets; the preparation of native foods appears on community college curricula, perhaps even at higher academic levels! Specialist Cain would be gratified at all this.

But among all Bugs' talents and expertise in natural science,

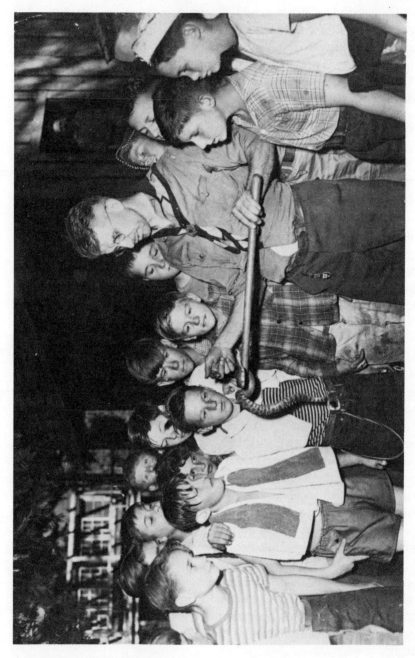

B. C. "Bugs" Cain with rattlesnake (Boy Scouts of America photo).

the one demonstration that brought him greatest fame was on the rattlesnake. It was his special mission to convince people of the east bay, not just his scouts, that this maligned reptile was not only useful in the balance of nature, but also docile and inoffensive if properly treated. And he generally made a good case until the famous incident.

The late Ray Schultz, lifetime Oakland scouter, liked to describe how Cain treated rattlers encountered on scout hikes, occasionally in the Oakland hills but more often at Camp Dimond O in the Sierra.

A raised hand from Bugs brought an immediate halt and silence as soon as the rattler was spotted. A correctly shaped stick would be found and the snake gently picked up and balanced on it. After a while it would be transferred to Bugs' shoulder while its principal characteristics were pointed out to the transfixed youths. Then it would be taken gently by hand and set free at the edge of the trail.

Another wildlife encounter even more awesome and formidable than the rattlesnake was almost guaranteed every Boy Scout who spent a week or more at Camp Dimond O—bears! Ample warnings about leaving food available overnight or flirting with these mighty and nosy neighbors were part of each scout's briefing at arrival in camp. But can you imagine controlling a bunch of tenderfeet from the city who had to leave their candy bars and other snacks hidden in tents and under sleeping bags for late night snacks?

As the chief nature man, Bugs had given his share of bear warnings to the boys. Secretly, like some of the older, experienced, and mischievous scouts, he liked to see bears in camp. Besides, his first avocation was photography. It is unfortunate that those snapshots of boys versus bears all seem to have vanished! Yet never a scout fell prey to a harrassed bear.

Almost any high Sierra camper could have a bear experience in those days; such encounters are still not rare, though the rangers have discouraged bears from campground foraging. But the gentler wildlife experience with naturalist Cain, as recently told me by Ray Sutliff, a veteran scouter, was unique.

A favorite hike of Bugs and his boys was to Inspiration Point overlooking the Grand Canyon of the Tuoloumne. Here there were deep fissures in the high cliffs. It was just the place to present Sierran geology and the gruesome example of man's despoliation of a magnificent canyon—Hetch Hetchy Dam.

Then came Bugs' big surprise. It would suddenly change his scouts from contemplating the awesome and sublime works of nature to watching close-up action. Their leader produced from his pack a roll of toilet paper and tore off tiny pieces, casting them out upon the rising air currents. Pouf! Pouf! Something would flash by and the papers would vanish! It seemed like a trick of magic to some of the boys.

Naturalist Cain made a few pertinent comments about lack of keen observation. Then one or two boys detected the little acrobats that snatched the papers, though they did flash by at incredible speed. Others caught sight of them high overhead, moving with a wing-flutter pattern unlike any other bird they'd ever seen. Raspy notes filtered down to the observers on the cliff. These were swifts, probably of the white-throated species. Whether they added the bits of paper to their nests in the rock fissures or simply played with them as some swallows are known to do remains an unanswered question.

One wonders if Bugs Cain by himself conceived this unforgettable demonstration or simply adapted it after reading of similar behavior by swifts or swallows somewhere else in the world.

Rattlesnakes, together with other snakes, lizards, amphibians, a few birdskins, and other native materials often accompanied Cain when he went out for a talk demonstration. Public and parochial schools, women's clubs, men's breakfast and luncheon clubs, and Sunday schools wanted this popular figure. The Boy Scout Council didn't object to this as he gave nearly all his waking hours, weekends and evenings included, to his mission in life. They called it "nature study," but nowadays it would receive more impressive names like "ecology" or "environmental awareness."

On one fateful occasion the program chairman of the Lake Merritt Breakfast Club had invited Cain to speak on their thirty-minute program and asked him to emphasize snakes. This didn't require much preparation on Bugs' part. He showed up with several portable screened snake boxes, including one with his favorite Pacific rattlesnake.

Bugs led off with a harmless specimen, his large gopher snake—the large yellowish brown, blotched reptile that is often mistaken for a rattlesnake and killed on sight. He then unlocked the rattler's box and reached with his snake hook to bring his pet into full view. Attention was rapt except for a couple of chairs at the speaker's table being pushed a little farther from this daring snake handler.

What happened next cannot now be accurately reported. Bugs apparently had transferred the rattler to his arm and had begun to point out its physical characteristics and good nature when some movement or sound alarmed it. Wham! There was a rapier-like strike, and before his astonished audience Bugs became a rattlesnake victim. There followed a stunned silence; then voices rose in concern.

Cain must have always considered this sort of mishap a possiblity. First he had to reassure the club members that it wouldn't be fatal and beg them not to be too concerned, as he returned the rattler to its box. Then he announced that he would drive himself to the hospital. A veteran member of the Breakfast Club recently questioned about this couldn't remember whether Bugs even applied a tourniquet or other first aid to the wound.

Now Cain the scientist and nature photographer took over. At the hospital someone helped him carry his heavy bag of expensive camera equipment. With the first discoloration and swelling of the affected arm, he managed to get a close-up and more pictures at intervals as it swelled to balloon-like size! In a day or two he was back at the Bug House caring for his unpredictable pet along with his other duties.

So many rattlesnakes were rescued from unlikely places or dangerous situations in the bay area and brought to Bugs that he found another crotaphile* to collaborate by boarding some of them. This older man was a rather singular figure who rode a motorcycle about town. Besides packing some of his pets in a sack or box on back of the cycle, he usually carried another snake under a large floppy cap. This rattler, he'd tell casual observers and acquaintances, was fully loaded and cocked like the others, but a few persons in his confidence said that he kept this specimen defanged!

In the 1930s while exploring the Pinnacles National Monument in the inner coast ranges east of the Salinas valley, naturalist Cain and his scouts made a rather sensational discovery of a yucca night lizard. This tiny, fragile lizard hadn't previously been found

* A word coined by some snake lovers and derived from *Crotaphalus,* the large genus of North American rattlesnakes.

north of the Mojave desert and Fort Tejon, announced Dr. Robert C. Stebbins, noted herpetologist at the University of California at Berkeley. After this incident, teams of "herps"* combed the south coast ranges and found a few more populations of this elusive creature inhabiting the duff under fallen yuccas and digger pines.

Cain's leadership of boys at urban parks, college campuses, or bay shorelines, his repertoire of bird songs and calls, and his techniques of snake display stamped him as a colorful, effective leader and teacher. His talent for imparting a deep appreciation of the natural world and for instilling in boys a sense of social ethics and keen powers of observation and communication didn't gain widespread recognition at first.

Star-finding or preparation for the astronomy merit badge, whether under the makeshift planetarium in the Bug House or out under the heavens on a clear night, became far more than mere identification of celestial bodies. Bugs' interpretation of the plan of the universe left his students, including any parents present, with a sense of awe. A sermon by the most gifted clergyman from a local pulpit could not have implanted a deeper feeling of mystery and wonder in a boy or left him a better boy or man.

Most successful leaders or public figures keep a ghost in the closet—a habit, weakness, or vice they would rather forget or keep concealed. Bugs Cain, in spite of his exemplary life and unquestioned authority on natural science subjects, had to live with such a ghost.

Bill Gracie, an Oakland businessman who recalls his association with Bugs and how he "survived" the dreaded bird badge test, knew about this "ghost," as did a few others among the older scouts and staffers.

Bugs had confided that although he'd once had a few swimming lessons, he had developed an aversion to entering any water over four or five feet in depth. For a leader of Boy Scouts, where every boy must swim in order to become a First Class Scout and to make the coveted Eagle rank, this was a sad hangup. Each time he emerged from the Bug House on a warm day, there were happy, noisy boys cavorting in the Dimond Camp pool. Some of his own protégés were sure to call out, "Hey Bugs, why don't you join us?" Clearly, something had to be done about this embarrassing situation.

* Herps is a colloquial term used among herpetologists.

Quietly Bugs sneaked down to the YMCA and took a few swimming lessons. Determined efforts finally got him to the stage where he could both stay afloat and cover a short distance. He decided he was ready for the "hour of truth." Another busy summer season was about to begin at Dimond Camp. If he could appear publicly and manage to get across that pool, he would put an end forever to those whisperings and jibes.

Came the day of reckoning. Several of Bugs' own protégés were scheduled to pass their swimming tests in order to make First Class rank. One worried boy who knew of Cain's aversion to water drew a comparison between his own fear and reluctance and that of Bugs. That was it—this patient, affable man had been goaded into action.

The aspiring scout candidates were lined upon the rim of the pool awaiting a signal from the lifeguard. Then who should appear on the scene but naturalist Cain attired in a swim suit. Amid cheers and a few taunts, he jumped in and swam clear across the pool—not too smoothly, but well enough to redeem his reputation and to encourage that reluctant boy who, incidentally, also passed his swimming test. Probably few of those present realized what guts it took for Bugs to overcome his lifelong fear of deep water and to prove it by that public performance.

In 1950 came a mortal blow at the height of Cain's popularity and achievement. The Oakland Council of the Boy Scouts decided to sell Dimond Camp to the Oakland school department. A chorus of protests arose from scouts and scout leaders of all ranks, but the council wouldn't reverse its decision. Use of Dimond Camp was shrinking, they claimed. Housing tracts were crowding in around the camp's perimeter. They'd be better off taking the generous price for Dimond Camp and buying a close-in wilderness camp.

So Dimond Camp was sold and a site for Los Mochos Camp out in the Livermore hills was purchased. No longer could city boys hike or take a local bus from their homes to camp whenever they felt like it.

Cain was no longer needed as a nature counselor except during weekend and vacation campouts at Los Mochos or the more distant Dimond O in the Sierra. But there was plenty of work to do in routine scout organization and paper shuffling.

Bugs tried this life of a regular scout executive, reporting to the new downtown offices. But his heart wasn't in it, and he severed his ties with the Boy Scouts of America after twenty-six

years of distinguished service. He tried a job as a student counselor for a short time but, like an animal torn from its habitat, he
couldn't seem to find another niche. He died by his own hand in
the spring of 1951. The youth of the east bay lost a true friend and
a gifted teacher and interpreter of the natural world around them.

This man must not be forgotten, was the reaction of a generation of scouters, grateful parents, and various associates of Cain.
An innovative Oakland park superintendent, William Penn Mott,
Jr., who had managed to establish a full-time park naturalist
program in 1947, came up with the right answer. Build a natural
science center close to the popular duck feeding area in Lakeside
Park and name it for Brighton C. Cain.

Contributions poured in from many quarters. The well-
known bird photographer Laurel Reynolds gave a benefit film
showing, and Harry C. Adamson, a noted waterfowl artist whose
early drawings had won Bugs' praise, donated a painting as a
door prize. When the committee was still thousands of dollars
short of its goal, Bill Mott enlisted the aid of the Oakland Rotary
Club and finally extracted $10,000 from the Oakland City Council
to reach the goal.

Today the memory and the spirit of Bugs Cain are perpetu-
ated by the Rotary Natural Science Center with its B. C. Cain
Memorial Library containing many of his books. Since its dedication in 1953, many a Boy Scout has benefited from the study skins
and other Bug House treasures housed in the center to prepare for
his merit badge examination. A new generation of young naturalists, both boys and girls, have found inspiration in studying or
assisting the park naturalists in this center dedicated to a beloved
teacher and leader they never knew in person.

The Nature Lady: Amy Rinehart

A LOUD KNOCK on the back door interrupted the breakfast of the Rinehart family in the ample kitchen. Dr. Rinehart arose, strode quickly throught the intervening passage, and opened the door. The caller was a miner from Gibsonville who had tied his sweaty horse to the back fence. His face wore a look of concern as he delivered a message to the doctor. Dr. Rinehart hesitated, then said, "I'll get there as fast as possible, Sam. Mrs. Simpson here might have her baby today, but I guess the women can handle it if I'm away.

"How would you like a ride to Gibsonville, Amy? Just had a bad accident in the shaft there. I promised to get right over."

Ten-year-old daughter Amy had already excused herself from the table and dashed upstairs for her boots and warm coat. It was 1890 and spring had come late to La Porte, once known as Rabbit Creek. There were still snowbanks in the woods and the always bad roads were now even worse with mud-filled chuckholes.

Sandwiches had been prepared quickly for Amy and her

father, "Doctor Mike," as his intimates called him. The doctor always carried extra bottled spirits for his own use on such a trip. Driving with a wise horse had its advantages in those days as the beast usually knew the way home.

The faithful horse was harnessed by father and daughter working together, and the familiar Rinehart buggy was soon passing the rocky craters of the early Rabbit Creek mining activities and heading northeast toward Gibsonville. Amy began a rather erudite monologue about her current reading in natural history and California history, and about wildlife she hoped they would see that day. The doctor enjoyed her company.

The road to Gibsonville took some concentration on the doctor's part; it was the sort that terrified strangers from the flatlands. But this was a joyous outing for Amy who, with her father, had previously survived this and many similar roads. She could take time to recognize and remark about the successive banks of trees and shrubs they passed—red fir, lodgepole and western white pine, manzanita, mountain lilac, dogwood, and others. She identified birds such as mountain quail, flicker, nutcracker, and red-tailed hawk. Her vision was always twenty-twenty, and she had keenness of hearing to match.

The mineshaft accident at Gibsonville had been a bad one. Doctor Mike would have bones to set, maybe even an amputation, though he muttered about how he hated those. For Amy this meant hours to prowl the empty lots and nearby woods, locating birds and seeking new plant species. Her only commitment was to check the horse and buggy now and then.

Amy was beginning to match the birds she recognized with their voices, a skill she learned on her own. Guidebooks, if any, were scarce. As for any personal help from her mountain neighbors, it is doubtful there was another resident bird watcher except for the older men and boys, who knew where to find—and bag—band-tailed pigeons, grouse, and mountain quail. With mountain plants it was easier. The earlier settlers had passed down the common names of herbaceous plants and shrubs they used for food and medicine. Where had they acquired this store of knowledge? From the local Indians who had used them for countless generations.

During Amy's girlhood some of the Maidu people were still following the old ways. They came through in family groups, digging bulbs and harvesting berries in their respective seasons, or gathering bark and grasses for fishnets and basketry. Some knew Doctor Mike by reputation, and if he stopped his buggy by the roadside, he and his curious little girl would try to communicate with these Maidu. All this Indian lore was added to the growing store of knowledge in the child's brain to be passed on to so many others in later years.

The myriad of herbaceous annual and perennial plants not named for her by local people Amy would carefully collect fresh, then sketch them or even press some for later identification. She wouldn't long be satisfied merely with local or Indian names; she would eventually insist on identifying them by family and scientific name.

What about the early schooling of this budding child naturalist? There was an elementary school in La Porte, but Mrs. Rinehart apparently didn't regard it highly. An educated, cultured woman, she took the responsibility for instructing Amy in the three R's, and probably imparted far more knowledge beyond the basic needs.

Then came the year of the big decision. Amy had completed the elementary grades in her home-taught curriculum and was ready for high school. That was a luxury few of the mountain children in small towns could afford. The nearest high school was many miles away.

Mrs. Rinehart argued that they must move to Oakland. Many aunts, uncles, and cousins lived there or in the vicinity. Amy would get the education she deserved and a wider range of social contacts. Her mother had always resented the uncouth drinking companions the doctor brought home.

Dr. Rinehart liked his circuit-riding mountain practice, despite the rigors, risks, and meager monetary rewards. He declined to give this up for the comforts of city life and a more lucrative practice. So Mrs. Rinehart packed up and moved with Amy to Oakland.

How rewarding this new life must have been, with science and history courses and access to a real city library. I don't know if or how often they returned to visit Dr. Rinehart and friends and neighbors in La Porte. Soon after leaving high school Amy began to support herself by selling subscriptions to magazines.

Amy entered my life sometime in the mid-1930s when we met on a hike with a local botanical society. A learned professor from the university might have been the leader of the day, but Amy

Rinehart was a most ready and voluble volunteer assistant. Her one failing was that she couldn't confine herself to the subject and purpose of the trip, plants. Everybody within earshot had to pause for the song of the wrentit, Bewick's wren, thrasher or lutescent (now orange-crowned) warbler if it happened to be in chaparral in early spring. Then there were close or distant geologic features which demanded recognition and description. It didn't exactly make Amy popular with the official leader of the trip.

This walking encyclopedia of natural history was well into middle age by that time. Neither physical appearance or attire ever concerned Amy, who tended to be on the heavy side and probably had never visited a hairdresser, at least in those mature years. High walking shoes, long skirts, a sweater the worse for long wear, and a long heavy coat of ancient vintage with bulging pockets—all marked Amy from afar on a field trip. For meetings, conferences and social dinners she might make minor changes in wardrobe.

Lunchtime on the trail always brought a motley display of food from Amy's knapsack or handbag. She often carried both. A leftover meat sandwich might assail nearby noses while many heads would turn away as she joyfully consumed black bananas and half-rotten apples or grapes. We often wondered if it was some lean days in her past or her present income that caused her to take such risks with food. At least she had learned not to offer to share with others.

But Amy's eccentricities were temporarily forgotten when she heard a bird call or song and gave an imitation as encouragement if the bird didn't continue. She had that ear for perfect pitch that enabled her to imitate with accuracy. Her enthusiasm over each new wildflower, no matter how insignificant to the average viewer, became contagious. Her style of introduction reached all ages, especially children, for whom she had a special store of terms, comparisons, and stories. It was easy to understand why she served many years as nature counselor for the San Francisco Girl Scouts at their camp near Lake Merced.

If Amy pinched on food and clothing, it was probably in order to spend more on travel. Since I always owned an old car and had time for a trip but not much money, it was by carrying Amy and her friends to distant parts of the state that I learned California history, and much of the field botany, ornithology, and other lore I would cherish and use.

Expeditions with Amy required careful planning. Amy Rinehart was a devoted clubwoman, believe it or not. I suspect she attended conferences chiefly to introduce or support all votes and resolutions on conservation measures. Conservation was less complicated then.

A stuffy conference with much sitting and eating had to be combined with a field trip in that general region of California. Only friends who felt likewise were accepted for the trip. Amy did allow a concession: they could make reservations in the nearest cabins or lodges while she and I, once away from the conference, would unroll our sleeping bags at a campground.

One memorable trip in the 1930s that began with a club convention in Los Angeles was more difficult for me, the driver-guide. Lacking any real expense account, I had to find a cheap hotel and a safe place to park the sedan full of camping gear. Amy had to pay the price of a room and banquet at a first-class hotel. But in the 1930s a single man with a little experience could get by in a large city on three dollars a day. Local zoos, parks, and museums were free if you could reach them, and I knew all their locations.

Death Valley National Monument was the field goal once the women were free of the convention. Five of us bravely set out over Foothill Boulevard in the old jalopy. After a long stop at Hunting-ton Gardens, we actually got over Cajon Pass to Victorville for the first overnight. Readers who have glimpsed the width and grade of sections of those roads that remain on canyon sides opposite the modern highway may imagine what bold adventurers we really were.

It was somewhat after dark the next day when we rolled into Furnace Creek Ranch, principal oasis in the valley. Here we deposited three women with their luggage at their cabins and then moved on to the campground. It wasn't difficult to select a good site for two sleeping bags. There was plenty of space at Death Valley in those days. More out-of-door enthusiasts and nature lovers would have visited this desert wonderland, but they lacked the price of tires, gasoline, and a few travel necessities.

It was up at dawn for bird finding whenever you camped with Amy. She did offer to help with breakfast, but her knapsack was bulging with leftovers from the last convention banquet. This would be her second day of living on these leftovers. "That waste of food was simply appalling," she would say indignantly. "My

mother taught me that to waste food with people starving somewhere was criminal."

The rest of the party was picked up at a more respectable
hour, and we set out for the popular landscape features within a
day's driving time of Furnace Creek (a loop that now would take
but two or three hours). The Salt Ponds, Badwater, Artist's Pal-
ette, and Zabriski Point were major stops. The third feature, called
Artist's Drive in those days, was a rough, one-way road through
spectacular narrow canyons. Amy, never having owned an auto,
would urge me to try the most forbidding road anywhere we
happened to be.

The old Chevy finally rebelled on a steep pitch and boiled
over. This didn't worry Amy, who immediately took off to look at
rocks and plants. Fortunately the motor cooled and I filled the
radiator from the reserve can on the running board (in those days
we carried spare gas, oil, and water). We did return to Furnace
Creek by dinner time.

Scotty's Castle and Ubehebe Crater were absolute must-sees,
announced Amy the following day, seconded by her companions.
That meant more than thirty or forty miles of sand and gravel road
from Stovepipe Wells in an overloaded car. I protested. They
insisted. I still shudder when I remember, but somehow we made
it. I couldn't afford the admission price so I waited outside,
watching birds and soaking my feet in a cool stream. The women
finally emerged, ecstatic over the mansion and its furnishings.
Fortunately the return trip was downhill.

A pause at Stovepipe Wells, then coming under seige from a
desert sandstorm, gave us an opportunity to refresh ourselves and
the radiator, and to refill the water can. How fortunate we did.
Long before old Chevy got us up to Towne's Pass (close to 5,000
feet in elevation) it was groaning and wheezing. Finally it again
rebelled and boiled over. Only the contents of our emergency can
cooled it down and got it running again. Our drinking water
would have to be used at the next boilover.

Matters worsened from then on. The road to Pannamint
Springs and Darwin, full of chuckholes, climbed and dropped
over what seemed an interminable succession of small ranges.
Darkness came on abruptly. Despite cooling temperature, Chevy
had boiled and boiled, and consumed all of the drinking water.
We must be nearing Darwin, we agreed, but there was one more
short steep grade. Chevy gave a last rattle and cough and quit
cold, with the summit dimly outlined just ahead.

My options were few, my responsibilities great. Should I walk to Darwin and engage a tow truck for which I didn't have adequate funds? Should we push it off the road and camp overnight in and about the auto? PUSH—the magic word rebounded in my brain. Our horsepower having failed, why not try womanpower? All four women were willing and pushed like veterans. Somehow the motor started and up to the summit we crept.

In a blaze of light below lay tiny Darwin. We greeted it as starving, thirsty, lost prospectors might have. Dinner at the local cafe was a celebration of relief. Three women even found rooms, and Amy and I slept with the scorpions, rattlesnakes, and kangaroo rats. The remainder of the journey back to Oakland was uneventful by comparison.

Another journey with Amy in the late 1930s was just as unforgettable, though very different. It was a homecoming to her birthplace at La Porte. I could bring my wife and we would camp. We would first go to Quincy, where Amy had cousins and a very special botanic treasure to show me. We could camp on the cousins' property.

The highways to Quincy were good by the standards of those days, and the county seat of Plumas as colorful and friendly as it remains to this day. but the principal objective of our visit was up in the woods a few miles out of town, off what is now the Feather River Highway, route 70.

This side road, about two miles above Keddie Resort, was a cliff-hanger for a short distance, then ran past several homes of settlers and terminated above a vast, mostly dry meadow. This was Butterfly Valley.* Here we left the Chevy opposite the last residence and began hiking uphill through the forest along the remains of an old logging road. Despite the grade, Amy talked incessantly of her first trip here, of pioneers she knew and, of course, called frequent stops for new plants and birds.

Suddenly Amy gave an exclamation of triumph. There they were in small clearings in the yellow pine forest: thousands of pitcher plants (*Darlingtonia californica*), or cobra plants in local vernacular. They crowded boggy areas fed by springs far above. Each plant did suggest a cobra with its forked tongue and inflated hood. Amy flopped ecstatically among the first group and we did like-

* The Butterfly Valley botanic area in the Plumas National Forest at this writing may still be reached directly by this same road without the long hike; however, a new access and parking from the longer Blackhawk Creek Road is in the planning stage.

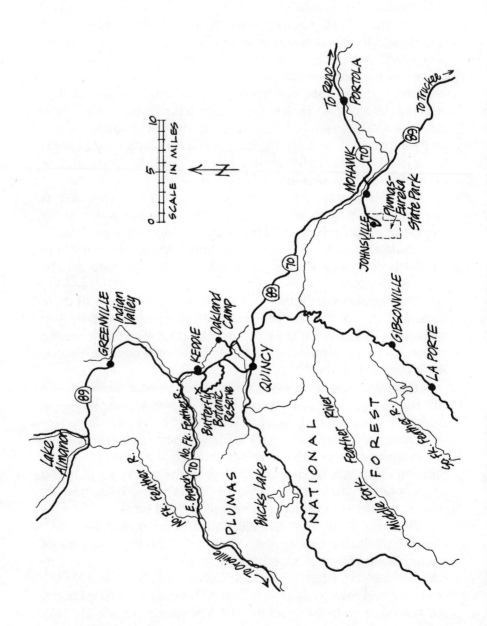

wise. She showed us how to cut across the base of a leaf to expose the small accumulation of insect remains, the recent victims of this insectivorous plant. In this way the plant makes up for a nitrogen-poor soil.

Before we left the bogs Amy also showed us a few tiny rosettes of the sun-dew or fly-trap (*Drosera californica*), which shares some of these northern California bogs with the pitcher plant. As we hiked back out she told us the story of Rebecca Austin, who had lived in Butterfly Meadow in the 1870s and learned so many internal secrets of this fascinating plant.

The next day we enjoyed a few miles of good highway on the Quincy-Truckee route before the ordeal that began soon after we turned off onto the Quincy-La Porte-Oroville road. This proved to be narrow, steep in places, and frequently hair-raising, with abrupt drops into deep canyons. The faithful overloaded Chevy made the usual remonstrances and boiled over. Unlike a desert trip, however, cold water for radiators and people was gushing along creeks and rivulets—many of which we had to ford.

Amy got much of her sleep while riding in cars, making up for note-writing into the wee hours of the previous night. We were just as glad that she stayed awake on a jaunt like this, though reminiscences and local history were being fed faster than we could digest them. As we neared La Porte she talked even faster as more familiar objects and landscapes appeared.

Suddenly the road leveled off and some shacks and ancient houses appeared. But mostly there were small, shallow craters strewn with boulders. These were the dismal heritage of early hydraulic operations before Amy's time. A few straggly trees and shrubs had since gained footholds among them.

Amy was at a crescendo of recollections when my wife interrupted. "Where do we camp?" she loudly demanded. "We don't want to camp right in town!"

"I'm afraid we'll have to," announced Amy with a sigh. "This is the way they left all the outskirts of La Porte. I think they will let us use the square. It's level and they used to have shade trees."

The town square was still there and available. It did have a few trees and a nearby water pump, but not privacy. My modest, tidy wife bit her tongue to refrain from scolding as she helped pitch our old tent. Little did she know what lay in store for us.

I don't remember if Amy had sent word of her coming, but it wouldn't have made much difference. Strangers making camp in the La Porte town square obviously were rare occurrences. First

came the smallest children who could toddle over and ask questions, then followed their older brothers and sisters. We felt like
magicians assembling and pumping up the portable gasoline stove.
The air mattresses and sleeping bags brought more wide-eyed
study. "These children just don't go camping and use such things,"
explained Amy. "They have the woods all around them!"

A rather shabbily dressed gray-bearded man introduced himself. Amy immediately recognized him as a former classmate from
one of her brief early stints at the La Porte School. The "under-
ground" telephone tree must have gone into action. Off went Amy
with him to meet his "old lady," and she didn't reappear until after
supper time. She had made the rounds of the town, rediscovering
old friends and neighbors. What gushes of conversation must have
ensued, matching Amy in intensity and endurance.

We decided to remain at our camp, although security wasn't a
concern in that day and place. A ring of children watched us
prepare and eat our supper. A friendly, loquacious older man
brought us some wood and insisted on building a campfire. Word
had circulated that I was a nature man interested in local wildlife.

This revelation about the stranger drew a succession of other
natives ranging from older boys to fathers and grandfathers. All
were anxious to tell about the big ones they had bagged over the
years: bear, mountain lions, and six- to eight-point bucks. It got to
be a contest, each topping the others' records. Occasionally I could
get one of these mighty hunters to talk about lesser game, and even
some local birds.

When Amy reappeared later in the evening this campfire ex-
change was still going strong, with nature man receiving far more
than he could give in return. Then the flow of input was gradually.
reversed as our indefatigable conversationalist took over, and these
men listened to her recollections of early mountain folks, etc. Good-
nights were said as they returned to the relative quiet of their
homes. The emancipated mountain girl had proved more than their
match when it came to story swapping.

But Amy was far from finished for that day. Out came the large
box of plants in damp papers hurriedly collected along the way.
They had to be pressed between the plant press sheets and properly labled. Next came the notebook where all the day's observations
and events had to be recorded. That gave me the excuse to join my
wife in our little tent.

It was up and off birding at dawn for our tireless friend. She did return for breakfast, but announced that she positively must see old Mrs. B— and the S— family who lived just up that back road. This we reluctantly agreed to and prepared to break camp. When Amy didn't reappear it was a matter of locating the tiny so-called "S— farm" and literally leading her to the car.

Continuing westward on a somewhat better mountain road toward Oroville, Amy resumed her reminiscences, but soon lapsed into a deep slumber. That was how she invariably compensated for midnight note-writing on her trips.

When in Oakland Amy made daily sorties from her modest home just east of the downtown area. These were often for a birding and botanizing trip somewhere between the Oakland-Berkeley hills and the San Francisco sea cliffs. Frequently it would be to give a nature talk at a school or club meeting or to attend some scientific meeting on the university campus in Berkeley. Older members of the university herbarium staff still remember vividly the many, many packages of herbaria sheets she brought there for identification.

The colorful early culture and society of the east bay and the personalities who still survived in her time must have demanded some of her attention. I regret that my interest then didn't lead me to take notes on her opinions on the literati: Jack London, Ina Coolbrith, Gertrude Stein, George Sterling, Joaquin Miller and others. As a teetotaler Amy must have been horrified at the habits of some of these people.

My wife Marion recalls one account of Amy's reactions to Juanita Miller, daughter of the poet Joaquin Miller. Dressed for some social function that both Juanita and Amy were attending, Juanita wanted Amy to accent her attire with some beads that Juanita was willing to lend to her. Amy remonstrated firmly and would have none of such non-essentials added to her dress.

An expense-paid tour of the eastern states, including many of America's historic shrines, was Amy's reward for achieving the top sales record for a certain magazine. I have often wondered if that publisher ever knew how much enthusiasm and learning resulted from that reward, and the number of people eventually reached and influenced by the recipient. That first long journey also lifted Amy's horizons and emboldened her to plan one far more daring.

The next and greatest travel adventure of her life was Europe! It was in the spring of 1952. She had scrimped and saved from her modest income to attain this goal. She also had written innumerable letters to museum curators, head gardeners, botanists, and ornithologists along her planned route. She traveled with a Swiss friend, a woman who had hiked California trails with Amy in earlier years. "You know, some of those cities are full of pickpockets, alcoholics, and people with loose morals," she observed. "I'll feel better with my friend along."

She was gone many weeks that summer. We received a couple of postcards but other mutual friends got detailed reports. We could imagine the amount of midnight oil she had consumed writing up each day's diary. Her itinerary took her from alpine flower fields to British gardens, from small shrines to the greatest museums and palaces.

Amy returned fairly bursting with new stores of information and accounts of her discoveries. Some of us were nearly overwhelmed, if a little envious, at the unstoppable flood of facts. Many of her true stories would be worth retelling had they been recorded, but one outshone all the others.

It happened when Amy was exploring a park on a large private estate in Switzerland. There, among many strange, exotic trees, shrubs, and flowers, she recognized a familiar American friend. At first she doubted her identification because this was about the most unpopular vine in eastern North America; its cousin was equally loathed in California. Yet here they appeared to have cultivated it along fence rows. It was poison ivy!

The honest botanist knew her duty and didn't shirk it. Probably she experienced considerable satisfaction in presenting her find to one of those curt, superior European head gardeners. She cut short her walk and hastened to the office.

Monsieur *Directeur* could not take this brash, garrulous American woman seriously. He had another name for this lovely vine that turned red in fall and had never poisoned anyone around there as far as he knew. This insistent American woman, still arguing, was thanked perfunctorily and gently but firmly shown to the door.

But Amy was not easily put down. This deceptive and dangerous American plant had to be unmasked and made known to all, she insisted to her Swiss friend and local hosts. The mayor and the newspapers should be informed. Then someone remembered the botanic garden in a nearby city. It was arranged to take Amy there with her specimen, a sample she had surreptitiously gathered and pressed in paper.

At the botanic garden, once ushered into the office of Le

Directeur, a dignified elderly gentleman, Amy triumphantly opened her folder and displayed her *Rhus toxicodendron*. Monsieur adjusted his spectacles and frowned over the specimen, then rang for his staff botanist.

M. le Botaniste arrived shortly, a slight, wiry, hardy-perennial type, took a careful look at the plant and pronounced it to be precisely what Amy had known all along! Both officials apologized for their ill-informed countryman and promised to communicate their finding to him. Furthermore, Amy told us, they announced they would search the entire canton if necessary to find and remove or clearly label any other growths of this insidious foreigner. There was no record of how many local Swiss had suffered from a strange rash and swelling of body parts, quite puzzling to the local medics.

Amy had only one purpose in mind for going to Europe. After her return, at an Audubon meeting, one of the women asked her if she had bought any clothes in Paris. Amy curtly replied, "I went to Paris to see the trees!"

Soon after her great adventure abroad, Amy's health began to decline, but she remained sharp and alert mentally, ready to cite facts, quote an authority, or relate some account. She positively had to attend that next meeting of the Audubon Society or the Cooper Ornithological Society in Berkeley. When she could no longer walk to the bus and from bus up to the campus, a good angel entered the scene in the form of Dr. Eric Reynolds, physician and ornithologist, who would transport Amy to the meeting, motivated in part by their long friendship and partly by his growing interest in geriatrics. The good doctor probably knew of her developing cancer. What kept Amy ticking so strongly was a mystery.

Our nature lady with the indomitable drive was finally forced to move into a convalescent home in the spring of 1958. She kept insisting she must get back home to sort her notebooks, herbaria, and other collections. Not too long before Amy passed away, I paid her a visit, bringing along a spotted fawn that happened to be in our custody. True to form, she began to lecture from her wheelchair to fellow patients on the habits of deer and other wild things. I know that some part of Amy's great knowledge and devotion to nature remains with all of us who ever rode or hiked California's roads and trails with her.

Mister Parks:
William Penn Mott, Jr.

How can one describe a man of so many talents, moods, and interests all focused on achievement, an incredible workaholic who could lay out a new park plan, discuss annual and perennial plantings with a garden club, play midwife to a sheep, extract large financial commitments from city councils or business tycoons, and still find time for a nature walk with his family—all in one week! Yet, that was typical of William Penn Mott, Jr., shortly after he assumed direction of the park system of Oakland, California, in 1945. Like some of my privileged contemporaries who were selected to work with this dynamic leader, I find it now difficult to understand how we managed to keep pace and serve him adequately in those thrilling, hectic times.

What was the status of Oakland's parks in the pre-Mott era? It

was indeed a precious inheritance, ranging from historic downtown plazas past Lake Merritt and Lakeside Park to the redwoods
and introduced forests of Joaquin Miller Park in the hills. The hill
parkland was blessedly undeveloped except for Woodminster
Theater, built into a lower slope by the Public Works Administration (PWA) and Work Projects Administration (WPA) during the
1930s.

The folks of Oakland flocked to Lakeside Park and Lake
Merritt for weekend and holiday recreation. There were rowboats,
launches, and sailboats for water-oriented sports, tennis courts
and lawn bowling for the athletic, wild ducks and swans for
families to feed, and band concerts in summer for music lovers.
What more could they want?

A veteran park superintendent who had served several decades, and a dedicated but not too imaginative board of directors
carefully maintained the status quo with a conservative budget.
Beautiful annual flower displays and some lathhouse and hothouse
specialties were cultivated by skillful, devoted gardeners, supervised by George Grimwood, a well-educated Scottish foreman.

A massive contribution was made annually to science and
research through official support of the wild duck roundups and
bandings. The record keeping and some labor were supplied by a
wealthy Piedmont sportsman, E. W. Ehman. An occasional rare
migrant or a longevity record got wide publicity and made everybody proud. In the 1930s I entered the scene as an enthusiastic
volunteer worker at the Duck Pond.

City fathers and the park commission had engaged a landscape
architecture firm to modernize the Oakland park system. Young
William Penn Mott, Jr., had earlier left his job as landscape architect
for the National Park Service to join this local firm. Mott, a graduate
of Michigan State with a master's degree from the University of
California at Berkeley had begun his career with the park service in
1933, serving as landscape architect at the San Francisco regional
office until 1940.

A new superintendent of parks was needed by Oakland when
Superintendent Lee Kerfoot retired in 1946. The name of William
Penn Mott, Jr., was among the applicants. Mott got the job.

The Mott cyclone soon struck the placid bureaucracy of Oakland's city hall with powerful lesser winds extending out across the
city. Changes and innovations had been indicated, but city officials
and personnel ahd expected them to be more gradual.

Bold, innovative captains and lieutenants would be needed to support this new general. Bill knew where to recruit his new command. Within a year he had chosen an assistant superintendent, Lynn M. F. Harriss, a brilliant landscape designer and U. S. Army reserve officer who couldn't entirely suppress his military discipline in the field. Then there came on board a gifted architect, Amadee Sourdry, who borrowed and adapted ideas from other progressive cities or countries. Little did city hall or other department heads suspect that Superintendent Mott would soon expand into the recreation and education areas.

Bill Mott had a plan conceived as a result of his years in the National Park Service. With the popular Lake Merritt Waterfowl Refuge feeding and banding operation already long established at Lakeside Park, and a part-time lecturer currently sponsored by a local service club, he would set up a park naturalist program. He had heard that the East Bay Regional Parks administration was considering a similar idea for Tilden Park, and Bill was not one to be scooped.

When word of this circulated through city hall there were the expected reactions. "What, hire a guy to tell people about the birds?" gasped an older councilman. "What will that fellow Mott think of next?" asked a financial advisor to the city manager. "If we have to have someone paid by the city to play naturalist, can't they find someone in the museum or the school department?" asked another.

"Don't worry about all that stuff you read in the papers," Bill reassured me during our second interview when I was taking the leap from a secure federal civil service job into this new career. "We'll just put you on as a ranger for a few months while I work on the council and the Civil Service Commission. You will actually go to work as a park naturalist right away—that is, as soon as you go through the Oakland Police School."

Mott's supreme confidence was infectious. His new nature man was soon off and running, wearing a makeshift uniform, an old U. S. Army campaign hat, and borrowing vehicles from sympathetic park staffers. The boss had a plan and the local press and radio stations were cooperative. Pictures of the park naturalist posing with new ducklings or cygnets; of Girl Scouts, Campfire Girls, Boy Scouts, Cub Scouts, Bluebirds, and Brownies visiting parks; or of garden club ladies planting trees began to appear regularly. The demands soared for the naturalist to meet youth groups at the duck pond or in various parks, lead a garden club tour, or speak at a service club luncheon.

Sure enough, within a year Superintendent Mott had the park naturalist position approved and set up. There would be the matter of a competitive examination, but the man already on the job usually had an advantage. In 1947 there weren't that many experienced, unemployed park naturalists. Only Cleveland, Ohio, in the entire United States had developed a full-time municipal nature interpretive program.

A great break for Mott, the interpreter and showman, came in 1948. California's Gold Rush Centennial followed by the centennial observance of California's admission to the Union in 1850. The staid city hall plaza with its token live oak tree and a few flower beds became the scene of a great transformation in the spring of 1949. A task force of men and machines, carpenters, masons, and gardeners personally supervised by Bill Mott, Lynn Harriss, and some architects labored day after day. Councilmen and bureaucrats emerging from city hall upon the scene shook their heads, passed critical comments, or walked across the street for a closer look.

When completion was announced and the press and photographers came, they saw a model of Sutter's mill, a stock corral, a Sierra stream, a 49er with his gold pan designed in flowers, and more—much more.

Another spectacular was taking place at Woodminster Theater in the hills. A lavish production, *Glory in the Land*, portraying California from Indians and the first missionary padres, through the Spanish-Mexican era, to Gold Rush and statehood, was drawing thousands of east bay people. It was free, financed by the state of California. Bill had even engaged a theater manager—a temperamental pro. The city fathers got box seats to enjoy it all, and they wound up applauding the show and their park superintendent. These celebrations continued into 1950 when the theme of the Woodminster spectacular was "Song of a City."

Another "first in the west," if not in the United States, was hatching in Bill's fertile brain. It was probably inspired by a children's zoo operated at Belle Isle by the city of Detroit. Arthur Navelet, a prominent local nurseryman, Russell Everett, a local artist designer, and one of Mott's own architects had each journeyed to Detroit to study this popular attraction. They agreed that something like it would certainly go over well in Oakland.

Plans for Children's Fairyland in Lakeside Park and the formation of fund raising committees were announced in 1948. This children's development would not only animate popular fairy tales, but would present live pets and domestic animals for city children to touch, another innovation in interpretation.

Response was enthusiastic from all sections of the east bay. Service clubs and social clubs all cooperated in raising funds for this exciting project. An organization would select its favorite theme piece, like the Giant Pumpkin or Willie the Whale. Park employees got into the act by building a set to install in Children's Fairyland after exhibition at the spring garden show. It wasn't easy, Bill and his planners discovered, to find carpenters who could put together a structure such as "The Old Woman Who Lived in a Shoe" from plans dictated by artists.

Where to find large domestic animals in a modern metropolis? Even the resourceful Bill Mott was temporarily stumped, but he finally had some leads in the suburbs, and dispatched the park naturalist to locate and bring in the sheep, goats, small pigs, and domestic geese called for in the nursery themes. A donkey, heifer, sea lions—even monkeys and macaws—would be secured for subsequent units whose themes demanded such animals.

Children's Fairyland opened in September 1950 with great fanfare and massive response from children and parents of the bay area. A woman of rare talents and charm, Mrs. Dorothy Manes, had been hired as director. So well did Dorothy manage Fairyland while Bill and his supporters promoted it that several years later Walt Disney came to Oakland and enticed away this gifted woman. Meanwhile, cities across the United States were busy opening their own versions of children's nursery theme gardens. The only sour note resulting from Bill Mott's sensational bonanza for the children of the bay area and the country came from some recreation professionals. It really was a recreation and not a park function, they proclaimed. This criticism didn't faze Bill at all. He adopted another traditional recreation function a few years later by building a puppet theater which was operated in succeeding years by a number of professional puppeteers.

About this time Oakland's headline-making park superintendent was elected president of the American Institute of Park Executives. It was typical of Bill Mott that his staff and co-workers should share this honor. The park naturalist began writing a monthly outdoor education column for their journal and the landscape architects also wrote and gained national recognition. There were

William Penn Mott, Jr. at Robinson Crusoe set, Children's Fairyland,
1955 (Oakland Tribune *photo*).

no financial rewards. Bill found himself traveling widely for
speeches and meetings. We all talked long distance as never before,
and Bill's secretary had to play a dual role, serving both the city and
the park institute. Fortunately, the mayor and city manager were
proud of their superintendent and never carped about this sharing
of staff time.

Mott realized it was now time to provide a home for the park
naturalist. An old locker room located between the men's and
ladies' restrooms outside the gates to the Lakeside Gardens had
been serving as the naturalist's office and makeshift classroom.
This fact, as graphically described by the superintendent at a city
council meeting, somewhat startled that dignified body and probably helped to move the issue. (How Bill Mott conceived and
promoted a real visitor's center is described in Chapter 3.)

But there occurred a minor crisis before Superintendent Mott
extracted from the council the final $10,000 needed to finish the
Rotary Natural Science Center.

"Mr. Mott assured us when we approved and prepared that

site for the center that he'd raise all the money from outside sources," proclaimed one councilman. "This is a typical Mott strategy," shouted another. "He did it before Fairyland was finished, and now he comes to us with the same story—so many public commitments that we look cheap if we don't pony up the difference." Little did the honorable council members know that it would happen once again before the Lakeside Garden Center was completed in the early 1960s.

Bill Mott lived dangerously. He loved challenges. More than once an experiment came close to costing him his position, professional reputation, or worse. The Easter animals for Kahn's Alley caused one such incident. The park naturalist, as usual, was deeply involved whenever animals were concerned.

Kahn's Alley is a cool, drafty shortcut between towering buildings directly opposite city hall and its plaza. "What a great place with all that pedestrian traffic for a live Easter display," announced Superintendent Mott at his weekly staff meeting. "Fairyland will supply some rabbits, guinea pigs, chickens, and things. Construction will make whatever is necessary to keep them in, and the naturalist will stop by when he can to check on them."

This was accomplished well before Easter Sunday. The papers published pictures, and shoppers stopped to admire and watch the children fondle the pets. Then it turned cold and rainy. A couple of animal lovers decided the Easter animals didn't have enough cover and heat and called the humane society, the press, and some city hall officials.

Superintendent Mott was summoned to the scene. He must have argued, told the complainants about the rigors of farm life, and refused to remove the display. A police officer was present, and the complainants demanded the arrest of "this cruel stubborn man." Mayor Cliff Rishell arrived at this point. A Mott supporter and a man with the gift of Irish persuasion, the mayor managed to cool the fracas and mollify the complainants. Mott didn't go to the police station.

There were other animal crises in those years of creative theme exhibits involving livestock. Sheep terrified by prowling dogs had leaped over their fences at city hall plaza and led park rangers and police a merry chase around downtown Oakland before they were rounded up. One Christmas season the sheep displayed at the Lakeshore Park nativity scene were harassed by boys and jumped the fence. They took the ramp up to the MacArthur Freeway, perhaps sensing that their farm home lay in that direction. It took the rangers, Oakland police, the highway patrol, and a few concerned citizens to herd them back to the set. In each case the pragmatic park naturalist had argued for higher fencing, but the big boss and his designers said no—it would spoil appearances.

On other occasions when the naturalist and his environmental supporters cried out against bureaucratic threats to the natural environment of the hill parks, Bill Mott threw all his weight on their side. Such was the case when city weed abatement people proposed to spray several hundred acres of the Oakland hills, both private and park lands, to eliminate poison oak.

Many desirable native shrubs would be incidental victims to such a blitz. Selectivity would be too much to expect from those crews. Besides, this much maligned poison oak yields nectar to insects, forage for deer, small berries for birds and rodents, even some honey. It is the principal erosion control on many a steep slope and, if these assets aren't enough, provides striking red colors in late summer and fall.

Superintendent Mott, a keen student of nature and the environment, was convinced of the advantages of poison oak. Addressing the city council, he managed to turn off the spray campaign. Instead, the park rangers only sprayed around picnic sites and along some trails.

Bill Mott also sided with his naturalist advisor and various nature lovers and environmentalists on a proposed all-out attack on the squirrels populating spacious Knowland Park in the east Oakland hills. The ground squirrels at Knowland were out of control, announced Alameda County health and pest control supervisors. They intended to open a poisoned bait campaign against them before they transferred bubonic plague or some other dangerous disease.

Not so fast, boys, replied Bill in effect. "The park naturalist and biologists we've consulted tell us the incidence of bubonic plague in this area is extremely rare, and that the Formula 1080 poison you are using could be picked up or transmitted to other small native animals."

Mott dictated a letter to the county: Knowland Park is off limits to your vector control crews. This brought dire warnings from the health and pest control forces, but Bill stood firm.

The Knowland Zoo, from its wild squirrels, deer, and quail, to its temperamental elephant, Effie, and an assortment of typical zoo animals housed in ancient cages, offered Superintendent Mott one of the greatest challenges of his Oakland park career. A small zoological society in the late 1930s had hired noted animal collector Sidney Snow, and had bravely assumed the mortgage and possession of the former Durant estate as a home for the animals of Oakland's small ailing zoo in Joaquin Miller Park. Director Snow somehow found food donations and free helpers, but the outlook for this zoo was dim.

By a master stroke of planning and persuasion, Mott had convinced Joseph R. Knowland, Oakland *Tribune* publisher and chairman of the State Parks Commission, that this 455-acre Durant estate should become a part of the state parks system. The commission agreed, and in July 1956 the city of Oakland assumed a lease and virtually total control of Knowland State Arboretum and Park. Trees from around the world had been brought to the property by Captain Frederick C. Talbot, and later occupants, the Deveaux and Durant families, had preserved them. However, the zoo always received more funds and attention than these stately old trees.

The zoo was developed on the lower southern portion of this large property. Sid Snow continued as director, and that led to occasional difficulties. Sid was an opinionated man who felt on the defensive over his name and reputation. He handled recalcitrant zoo animals with a stern hand and was ready to deal similarly with difficult or objectionable visitors. As a regular participant in Mott's weekly staff meetings, I witnessed some heated clashes between zoo director and superintendent.

The plans and drawings for a modern, sensational new Oakland zoo, drawn up under Bill Mott's supervision, blossomed in the local papers on a spring day in 1959. The price was estimated to be about $500,000. Neither the citizens' committee that approved it nor anyone else knew where all that money was to come from, except perhaps Bill. Construction on some sets was soon under way. Within a few months the unique entrance motif, a tall umbrella-like structure with a spiral viewing walk to house gibbons and spider monkeys, and a small elephant house were ready for occupancy. Just a few nights after Effie moved in, her old hay-barn quarters went up in flames.

Bill Mott achieved a record in park innovations and accomplishments that brought national and even worldwide fame to Oakland. This biographic sketch only emphasizes his determination to provide interpretation of the natural scene, some outdoor education, projects for youth, and a little history. In addition he was involved in physical and human park usage. For example, in 1960 he was granted a sixty-day leave to help Costa Rica plan a national park system. In the same year he was named to a fifteen-man board by the Department of the Interior to help plan future parks for the United States.

In 1962 a new horizon beckoned to Bill Mott, or, more precisely, was opened to him and his talents. It was literally just over the hills. The East Bay Regional Park District needed a general manager. William Penn Mott, Jr., was the favorite candidate. Could they lure him away from his Oakland position?

The East Bay Regional Park District at that time included most of Alameda County except for a few townships. Despite a great potential for expansion, there had been no major growth since 1958. An interim manager had taken over after the sudden departure of the last general manager. There was no civil service, only a union of field personnel, and no city hall to look critically over your shoulder lest you spend or commit too much money. An innovative general manager with a friendly board could move this park system to new heights. Bill Mott took the job.

The Oakland Park Department, from office and supervisory staff to the crews in the field and thousands of Bill's supporters, went into temporary shock. A department division head was appointed superintendent but found the pace set by Bill too rugged.

Another political bomb exploded in Oakland City Hall about six months after Mott's departure when the ever-watchful press revealed quiet efforts by Mayor Houlihan and a regional park director to discuss the transfer of Joaquin Miller Park, Woodminster Theater, and the Knowland Zoo to the regional park district. Although this proposal had been raised months previously, this time it came as a surprise to the Oakland Park Commission and to many park employees and citizens. "Looks like our Bill Mott wants to take half of Oakland's parks along with him to add to his new empire," remarked one critic. The whole matter was soon shelved.

Bill's assistant superintendent, John Peetz, took over in 1965 and did a good job of continuing some of Mott's policies and plans. But governmental reform forces which had long been advocating a merger of park and recreation departments eventually won a charter revision in Oakland that effected such a merger. Even the park naturalist's title was changed to city naturalist.

Once in the saddle as general manager at the regional parks, Bill Mott surrounded himself with top-notch officers to help bring about a new era in the park system. There would be territorial expansions, new installations, and a range of services far beyond the concepts of most park users, supporters, and even managers. Though the "idea a minute" an admirer attributed to Bill may have been an exaggeration, this man certainly projected new ideas at a baffling rate!

"I need a naturalist who is a good administrator, has a lot of new ideas for programs and exhibits, and can go out and raise money," said Mott to an advisor who had a wide acquaintance among park and junior museum naturalists. One name stood out among a handful of likely candidates. Christian Nelson was enticed away from the junior museum he had developed at Sacramento and made chief of the new interpretive department.

Participation and tactile experiences were guidelines in planning future naturalist-interpreter programs. Live and preserved specimens and slides were all right for showing at school classrooms, but these urban children had to be exposed to nature outdoors and to learn to look, listen, smell, and touch. The Little Farm built in the Tilden Park Nature Area in 1955 with funds from the Berkeley Kiwanians and built by the local trade school students was already providing such an experience for thousands of young visitors.

Naturalists Josh Barkin and Jack Parker responded to Nelson's ideas and plans. Parker's Junior Rangers were already repairing trails, planting trees, and improving habitat, many thereby earning merit badges or community service awards. Josh matched Chris Nelson and even Bill Mott in the hatching of new devices and ideas for better nature education.

Nature education at Tilden was really pioneered by the Oakland Public Schools, which had placed a science teacher and assistant in one of the old nature area buildings in Tilden Park some years earlier. City school classes should have the Tilden interpretive experience during school time as part of regular curricula, urged Josh Barkin, seconded by Mott and Chris Nelson. The former nature program should be restored on an even larger scale as some other school districts in California and the nation were doing.

So Chris Nelson and Josh Barkin made a round of school classrooms, mainly from the fourth to fifth grades, while Bill Mott went to work on the bureaucracies.

The campaign of persuasion was effective. Older primary classes from several cities began coming to the Tilden Nature Area within a year or so. The benefits to both children and teachers soon became obvious. Principals put these visits on their annual school calendars. Nelson had meanwhile hired a third naturalist, Richard "Dick" Angel. Dick later became the first naturalist at the new Sunol Regional Wilderness.

The facilities, however, were inadequate. One school naturalist tried to cope with thirty or more kids and parents on the trail, and funding was always tenuous. Somehow Bill talked the school district into getting out of the business, turning the program (along with their budgeted funds) over to the park district to be integrated into the new interpretive thrust of the park district. Two naturalists were assigned to each school class and new innovative facilities were put on the drawing board.

The Tilden Environmental Center, an award-winning structure designed in the round by district architect Irwin Luckman, was finally opened in 1974 during General Manager Richard Trudeau's administration. Its imaginative exhibits beguiled young and older visitors and a large classroom and patio provided instruction and staging areas for nature area explorations. Unfortunately, in 1978 the effects of Proposition 13, approved by California voters, curtailed many school field trips as well as crippling education and public services throughout the state.

While enlarging the East Bay Regional Park system by leaps and bounds, Bill Mott's visions and tentative plans were reaching other horizons. He envisioned a great ring or necklace of parks encircling San Francisco Bay, connected by riding and hiking trails under a new county regional park system. One can easily imagine how this proposal struck many local politicians and park-recreation bureaucrats who pictured themselves becoming subjects of such an empire. Some progress was achieved, however, in developing link trails in the east bay. Interestingly enough, in 1987 a bill was introduced in the state assembly to spend $200,000 on a feasibility study for such a trail system. Again, Bill was way ahead of his time!

"What? Move the botanic garden? That is completely unacceptable! How do you even dare to suggest such a thing, Mr. Mott? Why, it has taken twenty-five years to grow these trees and plants." Such was the gist of a volley of complaints and outcries that greeted Bill Mott's first proposal in 1963 to move the Tilden Botanical Garden from its small site in Wildcat Canyon to a 300-acre tract in Chabot Regional Park.

Garden director Jim Roof, a rough-hewn man of considerable talents in collecting, starting, transplanting and coaxing stubborn native plants to grow in Tilden Park, took a hard line attitude toward the establishment and his supervisors. Bargaining and conciliation were not among his skills. His reaction to Mott's proposal was predictable: "Over my dead body you'll move this garden," he said in effect. "I've cultivated and nursed it from a baby to a healthy, growing child. Nobody's taking it away!"

Despite his brusqueness towards strangers and gushy ladies in particular, Jim had a following of garden lovers among Berkeley women, and he enlisted three university professors. They quickly formed a defensive organization called Friends of the Botanic Garden. The friends gathered many signatures and picked up

William Penn Mott, Jr. at a new regional park (East Bay Regional Parks photo).

some political support. Some claimed that the revenue-yielding golf course wanted to expand into the garden parking lot and even into the upper area of the garden.

Bill Mott was forced to back down from this confrontation. Protracted warfare with the Friends would draw too much time and energy from his other projects. As for the Friends, they expanded into the California Native Plant Society, which now numbers chapters the length of California and has inspired similar organizations in other states. In an ironic sense, Bill was responsible for the creation of this active, influential group of native plant aficionados.

As yet there were no regional parks in Contra Costa County, and no naturalists to interpret the environment. Civic leaders, educators, environmentalists, and outdoor-minded citizens urged annexation to the East Bay Regional Park District. Bill, aided by Dick Trudeau and Doreta W. Chaney, and with the prestige of University of California President Robert Gordon Sproul (also president of the district's board), convinced the voters of most of Contra Costa to join the district in June 1964.

"Urban people and children must have access to a wilderness experience near home without having to travel to some national park or forest in the Sierra Nevada," preached Bill Mott. This came from the same man who also recommended developing mechanical parks, cycle hill runs, children's amusements, and swimming lagoons, to the horror of many environmental purists. Such a wilderness experience was provided at Las Trampas Regional Park. That spacious acquisition of wooded slopes and ridges south of Walnut Creek was given a wilderness classification in 1973. Above the growing suburban sprawl of Contra Costa County, it is a sanctuary for both wildlife and people.

Sunol Regional Park also was given a wilderness classification in 1973. Meanwhile a road extended up Alameda Creek to a site called Camp Ohlone. Coyotes and an occasional mountain lion foraged across Sunol Park; golden eagles and prairie falcons nested on its crags. Imagine the thrills encountered by a few urban boys who qualified for a week's stay at Camp Ohlone. Parents might visit if they would risk a rough dirt road.

There wasn't much shoreline or marsh in the park district when Mott took over in the sixties. A decade later Crown Beach, Elsie Roemer Bird Sanctuary, and the Crab Cove Visitor's Center would take shape at Alameda. Then Bill Mott, his directors, and the skillful chief of land acquisition, Hulet Hornbeck, saw a chance to acquire Coyote Hills on the edge of the bay just north of the Dumbarton bridge. The most significant fresh water marsh in the east bay existed there, serving as a holding pond for flood waters rushing to Alameda Creek. Cooperation with the county flood control district helped create this unique urban wildlife refuge partly hemmed in today by an urban community.

But it may have been the Ohlone Indian village sites that confirmed Bill's resolution to get Coyote Hills for the public. Archaeologists from many local universities had excavated the Indian shell mounds, laying them open to public discovery of cultures dating back at least 3,000 years. What a chance to show and tell the story of the bay region's first people. So Coyote Hills was added to the district's jewels just before industry and housing would gobble up the farm lands around it.

Followers of Izaak Walton always found a sympathetic ear with the general manager, who devoted many precious hours in planning new horizons and better catches for them. Lake Chabot, a water district reservoir in the hills above San Leandro (closed to the public by district policy) was a natural. Though off-limits to body contact usage, hordes of local fisher folk swarmed there at a historic opening in 1966 when Bill Mott had it stocked with trout that he got on sale. Only the blue herons and egrets nesting in the tall blue gums above the lake took a dim view of this turn of events. Naturalist-interpreters riding the cruise launch pointed out the herons and other natural features.

Bill planned recreation and fishing for three future Contra Costa reservoirs. Two would someday materialize. But there was one even larger planned project adopted, improved, and enthusiastically pushed by Bill Mott that didn't quite make it—the Clifton Forebay out in eastern Contra Costa County, a vast water impoundment that would have included district park land and offer aquatic sports. When it was beaten down by a few influential asparagus farmers and politicians, Bill felt hurt and rejected. (I can't say he was ever crushed.)

Once again there came a summons to new horizons—an invitation and challenge to innovate and develop across an entire state. Governor Ronald Reagan appointed Bill Mott Director of California State Beaches and Parks in February 1967. Within weeks he assumed office at Sacramento. In its "quantum leap forward," as a district writer termed it, the East Bay Regional Parks had more than doubled in size during the years of the Mott administration.

Now the Mott hurricane of change hit the bureaucracy of the Department of State Beaches and Parks. Personnel in the field as well as top brass in the Sacramento offices would soon feel the winds. Their reactions would vary widely.

"What? Women aren't allowed to compete for ranger exams? We'll get that changed right away," promised director Mott. This reclassification was soon put into effect. Soon charming female types with long tresses under their Stetsons would appear leading nature walks, conducting campfire programs, or checking campers. Any grumbled objections from hard-liners were soon silenced.

Then came another surprise ruling from the director. The seasonal naturalists who had covered most of the interpretive programs each summer would no longer be hired. Many brilliant, enthusiastic high school or college instructors, graduate students, and other well-qualified people had filled these eight- to ten-week jobs. Some had attracted large followings of state park visitors who would return each summer to the same park to accompany their favorite seasonal naturalist.

This startling decision was probably made some time before Bill's appointment, as he traveled about the state, dropping in quietly at various interpretive programs. Unfortunately he had attended one or two poorly staged campfires and encountered a seasonal naturalist here and there who he felt was enjoying a vacation at state expense.

"We will put all our rangers through a training course that will include interpretation of their environment," announced the director to a meeting of his upper staff. "Then we will create some regional naturalists to coordinate all this, get the visitor centers staffed, and so forth." (Trained docents eventually took over a major share of the visitor center staffing and performed other duties.)

Quite a bit of flak greeted this announcement, as top supervisors pointed out how busy their rangers were kept during vacation season with their present duties. But Bill was adamant. The plan went into operation immediately with the ranger staff given cram courses in nature. Many of the old-timers balked at this innovation, while other younger men and women loved the chance to perform at a new level and make more contacts and friends among the public.

Director Mott had no intention of leaving the situation like this. State park personnel at all levels deserved a proper training center on the order of the National Park Service centers. And Bill soon found a way to get it—tap the profits of the Asilomar Conference Center. This operation of model efficiency operating on state ground did actually yield substantial annual profits.

A modern training center took shape on the Asilomar grounds, complete with its own student dormitory. Justifiably, it became the William Penn Mott, Jr., Training Center. By this time the entry level ranger received a complete indoctrination ranging from the natural history of state parks to security measures and the ability to handle a sidearm. Unfortunately every Smokey Bear must be prepared to bear arms in emergencies, although routine patrols are provided by fully trained security rangers.

Director Mott's administration saw several new visitor centers or interpretive centers completed and opened and existing centers and parks provided with new equipment. He was fortunate in having as predecessor in the director's post Newton Drury, a professional environmentalist and park administrator, who with his brother Aubrey became noted for "Save the Redwood" successes. Together with Elmer Aldrich, a veteran naturalist serving as state recreation director, they had already picked sites and planned many of these visitor centers.

Bill Mott was dedicated to the idea of two major California history centers, one to interpret the Spanish-Mexican era and the other to portray the railroad history of the state. Needless to say, he achieved both of them.

Tiny, sleepy Old Town in San Diego became a Mexican village with restored buildings, period gardens, colorful bazaars, and lively restaurants. Annual fiestas helped to attract extra thousands of locals and tourists to this exciting reincarnation of Old Mexico.

The iron horse that brought commerce and hordes of tourists and settlers to the Golden State, and its right-of-way builders, from capitalists and engineers to toiling coolies, were offered in substance and by models and pictures for visitors at Old Sacramento Railroad Museum. This now-famous museum was achieved when Bill invited the Reagans to have dinner in an historic railroad dining car one evening. It worked. Fiscally con-

William Penn Mott, Jr. and Smokey (Oakland Zoo photo).

servative Reagan opened the state treasury for a raid by Bill to accomplish the project. It has expanded into a large, multi-level display structure. Another Bill Mott brainchild has brought pride in their state to generations of young Californians. Thank you, Bill.

It was back to his east bay base in 1975 when Governor Edmund Brown, Jr., took over in Sacramento. Many of us wondered why this environmentally minded administration could not overlook partisan politics and retain Bill Mott in his post. Despite all these changes in employers and in fields of operation, Bill Mott refused to give up his family home in an Oakland suburb, where his garden produce and steak barbecues had become a tradition. His supportive wife Ruth held down the fort and was liaison with their children. One son, John, became a California State Park Ranger, a source of pride Bill and Ruth could scarcely conceal.

For Bill Mott this meant only a redirection of his talents and incredible energy toward other projects. One such project was the California State Parks Foundation, which Bill served as president—it would benefit by increased membership and larger gifts toward more park acquisition. And who happened to be liaison officer for the state in the allocations from the federal Land and Water Conservation Fund? William Penn Mott, Jr., of course!

Through this busy schedule of speeches, inspection trips, and planning sessions, there loomed that other project, long close to Bill's heart—expansion of the Knowland Zoo. He dreamed of seeing this still-struggling establishment become one of American's major zoos. What an opportunity for a unique interpretation of the zoological world right here. He had found time to serve as consultant, so few of his friends were surprised when in August 1977 he became general manager—the unanimous choice of the zoological society's board of trustees. At last Bill had his zoo. Eagerly he seized the reins.

An eye-boggling master plan for the Knowland Zoo was unveiled the following year. One media story referred to it as "a 500-acre wild game preserve and amusement park." In reality it consisted of several biomes extending up the open slopes, featuring an African grassland, tropical forest, conifer and deciduous forest, plus a farm center near the summit. A cog railroad would take visitors to the upper levels as well as to an extension of the existing skyride. Innovator Bill Mott estimated that $30 million spent over the next fifteen years would bring this bold master plant to fruition.

A majority of the Oakland City Council was almost sold on the plan, but certain pragmatic city officials kept asking sticky questions about anticipated funds to maintain zoo operations. Even though they planned to turn over both the zoo and the surrounding estate to the society, they were committed to some annual support.

Then came the neighborhood uprising. "We don't want a Disneyland in our backyards," they cried. Manager Mott welcomed some top-notch negotiators to handle this vociferous, organized group. Former mayor John Reading, retired parks and recreation department head Jay Verlee, acting public schools chief Robert Blackburn, and some persuasive women members responded nobly. Certain critics were invited to join the board of directors. A compromise was reached—the hill development would be shelved. It was a cruel setback, but Bill Mott grinned and bore it.

Interpretation and education hadn't been neglected in all this master planning. Trained docents met school tours. A wildlife school under a gifted teacher accepted a group each week from the Oakland school system and became so popular that parents and teachers demanded a special summer session. Both were later terminated due to a school budget crunch. The summer school was later reopened by the society.

Bill Mott's talent for recruiting brilliant and dedicated staffers was again demonstrated when he made consulting veterinarian Dr. Joel Parrott the assistant manager of the Oakland zoo. Between them they managed to persuade the East Bay Veterinary Medical Association to install a small modern animal hospital at the Knowland Zoo. In 1985 Dr. Parrott became the manager of the zoo.

In the spring of 1985 what many of Bill Mott's supporters had dared hoped for did happen—a summons from the White House. President Reagan badly needed to rebuild the image left by former Secretary of the Interior James Watt and other appointees who seemed bent on selling off our natural resources. He knew that Mott could change a part of this clouded picture if installed as director of the National Park Service. Bill deliberated at great length over this invitation. He knew that reactionary elements remained in Washington and asked if he would really have a free hand as parks' chief. Apparently Reagan and Interior Secretary Donald Hodel assured him that he would. William Penn Mott, Jr., became director of the National Park Service in May of that year. What followed will certainly furnish countless media pages and material for several books. Already the physical condition, general employee morale, and public appreciation of the national parks have shown an upturn welcomed by most of the Americans who know and love this national treasure.

Peerless Teacher,
Tireless Traveler:
Junea W. Kelly

A GROUP OF WOMEN in colorful costume fluttered around a tall angular woman wearing a plaid skirt and beret on Shoreline Drive in Alameda. Some drivers slowed down to gawk. Binoculars dangling from necks were the giveaway. "Oh, that's just a bunch of bird watchers," the driver would say, and the car would resume speed.

"I have a surprise for you today," announced leader Junea Kelly. "Today we're going to look for rails at Lehi Torrey's place."

This was the equivalent of announcing there was a very rare bird on a nudist beach.

"What?" "At Lehi's place?" "Is it safe to go there?" A chorus of excited, fearful voices greeted the leader.

The mysterious Lehi Torrey, whose cluster of shacks and boat hulks dominated the McCartney Marsh on Bay Farm Island, was described by environmental writer Harold Gilliam as ". . . a lumbering bear of a man who seems to be an indigenous part of the natural scene. With a beard and a trident he would make a perfect tideland Neptune."

For years bird watchers, curious youths, and nimrods with guns had scrupulously avoided Lehi's property. A crude sign at his driveway proclaimed the place to be a "Teredo Control Research Station." The name "Lehi" had been given to a Kon Tiki type raft constructed there on which some adventurers had launched on an ill-fated trans-Pacific voyage.

"It's quite all right, ladies," snapped Junea with her customary assurance. "Elsie here says that Mr. Torrey has been protecting some of the rails and wants us to go over to see them." Elsie Roemer was a trusted friend and competent birder.

A short drive on the Bay Farm bridge over the tidal channel, and along a road between the marsh and some attractive truck gardens brought them to Lehi Torrey's guarded domain. A few women were still apprehensive as they took the boardwalk leading to the buildings past a large No Trespassing sign.

Lehi emerged from the structure he called his home and office and greeted them warmly. He even condescended to join them and to lead the way along his boardwalk over the tidal marsh. Fears were dispelled.

He called softly. A clapper rail walked out from under the boards, followed by another. His "marsh chickens," Lehi called them. And he described two other rail species, the sora and Virginia, which often took shelter there. His reputation with the lady bird-seekers—even with Junea—was secured.

Torrey thrilled the bird watchers with another announcement that morning. He was prepared to do battle as a one-man commando against the sinister forces that threatened destruction of his beautiful marsh, the birds, the rich truck gardens, and all the things Junea and her followers held dear. After this declaration, he was immediately hailed as a new member of the task force being assembled by Junea, Elsie Roemer, and many other defenders of the birds and the shoreline environment.

Before getting involved with the "Battle of Bay Farm Island" (title courtesy of Harold Gilliam), let us take a look at this remarkable leader, Junea W. Kelly.

Born of second generation German parents in Portland, Oregon, in 1887, this lively, curious, red-haired girl eventually found herself in San Francisco. There, in 1909, she met and married a prosperous businessman, G. Earle Kelly. They honeymooned in Hawaii, where she fell in love with the tropical vegetation. Back to the islands she went in 1917 to obtain a valuable plant collection for the Academy of Science in San Francisco.

Plants and the academy provided a welcome new interest for her when she was widowed in 1917. She became an assistant to the noted Alice Eastwood, Curator of Botany at the academy. Alice had personally rescued many herbarium sheets and records before the first academy on Market Street burned following the great quake of April 1906. Collections from California and other states and foreign countries were about to swamp this lone plucky botanist.

Junea gulped down botanical lore and collecting know-how from her mentor. After all, botany had always been her first love. Here at the academy she was actually handling exciting plants from many parts of the world—and to be paid for this fun! Though by this time she never felt pinched for funds.

But their common devotion to the academy and to botany couldn't convert two such strong-willed outspoken women into a harmonious team. It was time to sever relations.

A big break into scientific circles came to Junea on the opposite side of the bay when a World Geological Congress met at the University of California in Berkeley. She seized this opportunity to fall back on geology—always a lesser scientific interest. She knew her local geologic history and how to demonstrate her knowledge, so she became the interpreter and guide for the German geologists who attended the conference; fortunately she had not forgotten her ancestral language.

Lucrative, attractive opportunities seemed to come her way. Dr. Harold Bryant, popular naturalist and teacher on the Berkeley campus, became a National Park Service administrator and turned over to Junea his "Six Trips Afield." This course was an introduction to the natural sciences of the bay area. It called for a working acquaintance with all the birds the class might encounter, their calls and songs. This offered no problem to Junea. She was already a pretty competent ornithologist. Unfortunately, she had always been too busy to stay in college to earn a degree.

Junea in fact soon made such an impact on the local ornithological circles that she was elected president of the prestigious Cooper Ornithological Club and a fellow of the National Academy of Sciences! And she naturally became very active in the fledgling Audubon Association of the Pacific.

Junea Kelly's consuming passion for more knowledge of everything that grew, flew, walked, crawled, or swam, plus geology and meteorology was matched only by her communication skills. Learned professors and veteran naturalist lecturers, supported by excellent slides or films, often failed to equal Junea's powers of description. "What! Didn't I carry a camera? Heavens, no, there wasn't any time for picture taking," was a frequent Kelly retort.

Just imagine this insatiable seeker of nature arriving in the Canadian Arctic at Churchill on Hudson Bay just as the ice was breaking in June 1938. That was the first formal Kelly travel report I remember.

The little train that transported Junea north from Winnipeg through the stunted forests of blue spruce, balsam fir, tamarack, and paper birch could scarcely contain her as she spotted new birds, mammals, and plants along the right-of-way. The excited red-haired woman dashing from window to window or out on the platform must have puzzled the stoic Indians, Canadian laborers, and dour officials sharing her coach!

Suddenly the last wide-spaced, contorted tamaracks of the taiga gave way to the open tundra at Churchill. Brilliant patches of arctic flowers beckoned to her. Birds singly and in flocks flew alongside or over the train.

After the formalities of registering and stowing her baggage in one of the plain but adequate hotels, Kelly was loose on the tundra. Listeners thrilled vicariously as she named her first discoveries: there were eiders and old squaw ducks nesting around the tundra pools; ptarmigan strutting heedlessly across the landscape; screaming arctic terns and predatory jaegers flying overhead; and three species of longspurs foraging along the edge of the road. And the flowers! Junea became even more ecstatic as she portrayed five different types of vegetation, from a kaleidoscope of lichen colors, through a vast array of grasses and sedges, to brilliant saxifrages and heaths fringing the precambrian rock ledges. All this spread out so vividly before our eyes without a single screened image. Some listeners vowed they would follow Junea's steps to the arctic Eden, a wish realized years later.

Then came the first of a long series of annual adventures for students of the natural world of these United States—the opening of the first National Audubon Society's camp at Hog Island, Maine, in the summer of 1940. Who was among the first registrants (and must surely have been the outstanding student leader of that session)? Junea Kelly, of course. When some two score species of eastern warbler migrants arrived to puzzle even some eastern birders, she was first to recognize them and help the leaders point them out.

This was quite understandable to all who had come to recognize Junea Kelly's talents and keen powers of observation. Her carefully timed flights were observed from year to year. Someone in her network of strategically placed scouts told her a certain migration was imminent and off she flew: Point Pelee on Lake Erie, Hawk Mountain in Pennsylvania, Cape Cod in Massachusetts, or Rockport on the gulf. Junea would arrive at the nearest airport, get a taxi or phone a friend, and there she was with binoculars raised and notebook in hand recording the warblers, hawks, ducks, cranes, or even migrating monarchs.

World War II grounded Junea Kelly for a while. Bird seekers and botanists did not receive much priority on transcontinental flights or trains. With characteristic adaptation to circumstances, she became an instructor in nutrition and Red Cross first aid at Alameda High School. Now there was more time to study those spectacular shore bird movements on her own Alameda shoreline, or to bird at Lake Merritt in Oakland, or in the Oakland-Berkeley hills.

When the big guns stopped booming and the bombs no longer fell, Junea began making travel plans on a greater scale than ever before. She was soon hopping over oceans and continents in her widening search for new birds, plants, natural landscapes. Her circle of scientific contacts—ornithologists, botanists, and conservationists included those in war-torn countries who had survived to resume their careers.

What the devastation and disruptions of World War II hadn't done to wildlife and wild places in the Pacific, Asia, Europe, and North Africa, the economic expansions and exploitations that surged like tidal waves in the ensuing years threatened to accomplish. Professional and scientific study societies embraced new objectives in rescue efforts or even delaying actions to save wild creatures and their habitats. Many citizens' groups, impoverished natives, even hunters and fishermen, joined local, national, and international efforts.

Off to Upsala, Sweden, went Junea Kelly in the spring of 1950 for the International Ornithological Congress. Concerned scientists, men and women from many nations of the world, were consulting on how to save some rare or vanishing birds and on various other technical subjects. The exhilaration of meeting so many famous scientists so moved Junea that she returned to the very next Ornithological Congress at Basle, Switzerland, in the spring of 1954.

Junea W. Kelly, 1954 (Oakland Tribune *photo).*

Two such experiences might have satisfied the average American delegate for a while, but not Junea. Back to Europe she flew in the spring of 1958 to Helsinki, Finland, for the meeting of the International Committee for Bird Preservation. This affair proved to be too much for some delegates. Kelly's vivid account of the physical hardships so shocked the members of the Golden Gate Audubon Society that perhaps few took home clear recollections of the findings and resolutions she described.

Picture the delegates, many from temperate and tropic climates, turning out of their warm beds for a six o'clock reveille, a seven o'clock breakfast, and the morning assembly at eight o'clock and sitting on hard wooden benches in a cold, cold hall! Did those Finnish hosts assume the rest of the world lived by their rigorous style? All this hardship Junea described in a matter-of-fact way.

Meanwhile, discoveries south of the border had been added to Junea Kelly's conquests. A venture into Latin America in the spring of 1952 led her from Florida down through Mexico and eventually to Panama. Somewhere she must have acquired sufficient Spanish to make her wishes known—and very precisely, no doubt.

Barro Colorado, the famed "jungle laboratory" of the Smithsonian Institution, lies in the middle of Gatun Lake in the Panama Canal. Here she came face to face with spider monkeys, tapirs, peccaries, toucans, parrots, and parakeets amidst an array of new bird and mammal species, strange reptiles, and grotesque insects you'd hardly believe. Choruses of howler monkeys in the treetops vibrated the little cabin where Kelly tried to set down her daily notes and keep her precious field guides from mildewing overnight. And the vegetation! Junea had to stretch her incredible vocabulary in trying to picture it for her listeners back home. There was that baffling array of sky-reaching forest trees, some bearing brilliant flowers in the upper story of life "zones," the lianas and mosses draped so profusely, and the fascinating plants of the ground level or "under story."

And what was the impact of this supercharged, voluble Yankee woman on the resident staff at Barro Colorado and the several research students who were always present? It must have been profound and long lasting. It was almost twenty years later, again following Junea's footsteps, that my wife and I experienced a Barro Colorado adventure. In the course of conversation at the long mess table shared by all, we mentioned her name as a friend who inspired us to visit there.

"Oh, that woman from California?" replied an older staffer. "We'll never forget her! She'd be out before breakfast, then ask for a sandwich and be gone all day. One evening she asked for a good flashlight for a night walk, but we had to talk her out of that. You know they asked her to submit her notes for the Smithsonian Year Book."

Junea Kelly caught jungle fever—the sort that infects the brain with an irresistible lure. The next year she flew like the migrant birds she had studied down to Peru, Brazil, and Venezuela. Boats, canoes, and Indian guides were engaged to take her into the forests along the river systems. Animals that had thrilled her vicariously in past years became live subjects to swell the growing lists of "firsts" in her daily notes: hoatzin, cock-of-the-rock, fantastic humming-birds, sloth, jagarundi, monkeys galore, anaconda; a mounting collection of hard-won prizes. And the rain forest itself—that green ocean comprised of hundreds of species of trees and shrubs within each square mile! Even Junea was overwhelmed. It defied adequate description. Only some particularly flamboyant species could be recognized here and there. Once again Kelly had met her match.

Back home again, Junea began planning a Pacific and "down under" tour. Her distinguished birder greeter lists served her well in planning her itinerary. botanists, ornithologists, geologists, and other fellow travelers in the natural sciences had enjoyed Kelly-escorted tours afield to view the objects of their quests in Califor-nia. It was just a matter of getting in touch with them now. This time she would take along her devoted pupil and friend, Roberta Long, who carried a camera and insisted on taking a picture here and there.

All these people, places, and dates were nicely lined up before the team of Kelly and Long descended on Australia at Sydney in 1959. Soon sightings of kangaroos, wallabies, opos-sums, wombats, platypus, malee fowl, lyre birds, kookaburras, parakeets, and scores of lesser birds, plus some grotesque lizards, and ominous snakes were crammed into notebooks. Almost over-whelming was the abundance of gums and wattles, better known as eucalyptus and acacia beyond Australia. There seemed no end to their variety and range in size and appearance, so it appeared hopeless to even try to learn them all, confessed Roberta. But Junea, the scientist, dutifully described each species in her notes, pausing to exclaim with pleasure when she recognized one that grew in Golden Gate Park, on the university campus at Berkeley, or elsewhere on her customary beats back home.

The succession of friendly hosts and guides who greeted Junea and Roberta from Sydney to Melbourne probably didn't waste much time showing off their towns and cities, except for science museums, parks, or botanic gardens. The pace of this down under discovery tour slowed for a few days when they were honored guests at a remote sheep station north of Melbourne. Here, by contrast, they were exposed to the farmers' views of the 'roos, dingo dogs, emus, and vast swarms of parakeets that would consume the fruits of their labors.

Next came New Zealand, cool in climate but also alive with gracious hosts. Time was running out and the tireless team had to settle mostly for ordinary sightseeing, botanizing, and birding. This included birds like the flightless kiwi and weka, bellbirds and tui, thieving kea, and a host of lesser ones. There were towering forests of New Zealand beech, the *Pittosporums, Hebes,* and magnificent tree ferns she'd introduced in California parks. One of their biggest surprises, which Roberta later described, was a thriving forest of California coast redwoods.

Lest I have created the image of Junea Kelly as a figure always leading a group, embarking on a trip or plunging into an environmental brouhaha, let me relate the Hummingbird Account. It will reveal how dedicated and tenacious she could become once she chose to do a bit of serious observation and study.

One year in early January, just outside Junea's bathroom window in Alameda, an Anna's hummingbird selected a patio shrub and proceeded to build a nest. The naturalist saw this as an opportunity to keep an hour-by-hour, day-by-day record of her guest's domestic life.

First would come the finishing of the exquisite tiny nest cup, the interval of egg-laying, the days of incubation and then the exciting days of hatching and feeding through to the successful fledging of the brood.

How could Junea carry out this self-imposed nest watching commitment, yet take care of her classes and other outside obligations? The answer was simple—call in the "Kelly girls." A well-coordinated chain of female students took their shifts in the bathroom week after week until the great flight day of the two fledgling hummers. Junea and four Kelly girls had covered virtually every daylight hour from January 9 to March 5. A complete, uninterrupted record of a nest observation was made for science.

Trouble loomed on the home front in Junea's vast front yard

on the bay, long the outdoor laboratory for her bird students and for visiting ornithologists from around the world. In fact, two bays were involved—San Francisco Bay where it lapped Alameda's outer shoreline, and San Leandro Bay (once known as Oyster Bay), a connected inland body of water to the east.

Long before the advent of the Ohlone Indians and their ancestors with their tule rafts and bird nets, tens of thousands of shore birds and waterfowl had foraged along the shores and marshes of the peninsula that came to be called Alameda and around the inland bay. They were still arriving each year in late summer and early fall up through the years of World War II and well beyond that.

Sandpipers, sanderlings, willets, godwits, avocets, curlew, dowitchers, plover, and many others were there at each low tide, jabbing, probing, and pecking the bountiful mud flats for their sustenance. Cruising the adjacent shallow waters were flocks of mallards, pintails, widgeons, shovellers, and teal ducks, with canvasback, scaup, ruddy, and scoters just beyond, all feeding avidly, each according to its tastes and style. Shyer clapper rails and sometimes sora and Virginia rails poked their way through the pickleweed (*Salicornia*) into the sheltering cord grass. Long-legged egrets strode back and forth seeking smaller fish and other goodies.

When a threat in the form of a human, dog, or darting marsh hawk (harrier) came in view the shore birds rose in clouds, termed the "living sands of San Francisco Bay" by wildlife photographer Laurel Reynolds who filmed these scenes.

The tundra of Alaska and the northwest territories provided a summer home and nesting grounds to many of these shorebirds who with their offspring found their way back to these hospitable shores each fall. Most of the ducks had nested from forest lakes to prairie potholes, from British Columbia and Alaska to the mid-Canadian prairies, each according to ancestral patterns and specie habits. Some shore birds and ducks might extend their journeys southward along the Pacific Flyway during the winter, but come early spring the great masses would again head north toward the wide open lands of Canada and the Arctic.

The garbage explosion and the urgent demand for dump sites which had already doomed so many marshes and tideflats around San Francisco Bay now endangered an area Junea and other bird watchers had always deemed sacred. The Alameda city fathers approved diking for trash-filling in a section of San Leandro Bay within their jurisdiction. Some development might follow.

Junea and friends girded for battle, pounced on the mayor, the city manager, and each member of the council. They received evasive answers and an invitation to appear and state their case. Meanwhile the new dump reared its ugly head, displacing the former marsh and bird life.

The Kelly telephone grid went into action. From all over the bay region and other cities and states came protests from ornithologists, teachers, marsh ecologists, and plain bird watchers. These had little more effect than spitballs on the Alameda politicians who might have been deterred by a mass protest from Alameda citizens. The dump stayed and grew. Junea had lost her first round.

Emboldened by this success, big business soon threw out a new challenge to the bird protectors and environmentalists. It was proposed to fill in the tideflats along the entire length of the Alameda Bay shoreline to build modern apartment houses, homes, and a shopping center. A novel appeasement plan was offered those old shoreline residents who had set up howls over the loss of their view: a system of lagoons would be built between the new developments and their homes so they would still face water and could even enjoy secure boating sports—at least those who wished to stay and could afford it. Why, even the birds would find these lagoons attractive!

Again the Alameda bird and shoreline protectors and supporters rallied and formed a militant group to stop this new rape of their shores. This time Junea, recovering from that last defeat, didn't take a leadership role. The Utah Construction and Mining Company, through an alliance of cooperative politicians, bankers, developers, and masters in public relations, convinced Alamedans that this South Shore project would bring vast benefits. It was approved at a special election.

By the late 1950s thousands of tons of bay mud had been dredged, heaped, and packed to form this new South Shore. Blocks of luxury-type apartments were taking form. Then, true to their promise to outdoor and nature buffs, the developers spread beach sand the entire length of the shoreline except at the far eastern end, where natural saltmarsh was encouraged to reform— a concession to the bird lovers.

A miracle occurred that would soon disarm and eventually

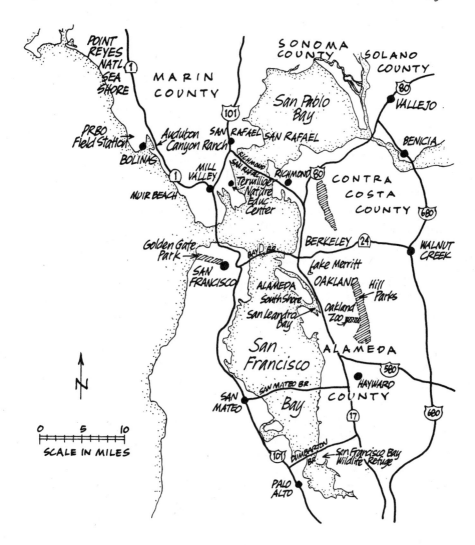

please the minority of die-hard protestors who had criticized the
South Shore project. The shore birds returned en masse to feed on
the reconstituted tideflats. Ducks, rails, and herons were again
seen on the marsh strip at the eastern end. Thousands of sun
worshippers from Alameda and nearby cities thronged to the
sandy beach on warm days, creating unforeseen traffic problems.
Eventually the East Bay Regional Park District took over the entire

shoreline, including the bird marsh, which was aptly named the Elsie Roemer Bird Sanctuary.

Junea and her friends and all the bird-seekers who came from near and far to bird along the new South Shore were not allowed many years to enjoy the status quo. The conspiracy of big business, politicians, and developers that planned South Shore was about to launch another coup—the battle of Bay Farm Island would soon take shape.

The lovely and irreplaceable McCartney Marsh across the channel from Alameda's South Shore would make an ideal residential subdivision. Shoreline Properties, Inc., godchild of the mighty Utah Construction and Mining Company, was seeking title from the city of Alameda "to replace this useless marsh and mudflat with a development that would raise the tax base of Alameda to benefit everyone."

Junea fairly exploded. Lehi Torrey stormed from the marshes to blast big business and politicians alike. An Alameda Conservation Association, led by a few determined citizens, was quickly formed to bring legal action against the sponsors of this preposterous proposal. One brave councilwoman joined them. College professors, schoolteachers, sportsmen, and ecologists fired verbal rounds. The Oakland Airport protested this new community close to the paths of jet liners. Geologists testified that a deep earthquake fault lay offshore.

The state of California became involved; the State Lands Commission, guardian of tideland grants to the cities, presumably had veto powers over such a project. Finally the Secretary of Defense was asked to prohibit the U. S. Army Corps of Engineers from granting the essential dredging permit. Appeals even went to Secretary of the Interior Stewart Udall because he was conservation oriented.

At that fateful meeting of the Alameda City Council in April 1965, a show of force mustered by the marsh protectors jammed the council chambers. But the chief voice of the opposition hadn't yet arrived; people were whispering and stealing glances toward the door. then Junea Kelly, convalescing from a broken hip, appeared in a wheelchair pushed by a friend.

The conservationists all got their turns to address the council: Junea, Lehi Torrey, the sportsmen, the Association, and some scientists all fired their salvos. Then came the mild-mannered spokesman for the developers who sympathized with the birders, boaters, and fishermen, but asked if the citizens of Alameda should be denied this bonanza in increased business and tax reduction for all? When the vote was called on the application, big business won by a council vote of three to two.

Junea was grief-stricken and numbed by this defeat. Her great physical strength and stamina had already been sapped by her accident. "I give up," she told some of her friends shortly after that meeting. "I've spent years fighting the good fight, trying to make the people of Alameda realize what a resource—what a natural treasure—they have here. Now they've beaten me for the last time. I'm through."

Soon the monster dredges arrived in the Bay Farm channel. Siphons spewed bay mud over *Salicornia* and cord grass, the homes of rails and saltmarsh harvest mice, the channels where ducks swam, and the shore where swarms of shore birds fed at low tides. It was an ugly drama to watch, this strangulation of McCartney Marsh. Lehi, the resident protector of it all had surrendered to the inevitable, taken a good price and moved away.

Junea's valiant battles, at least her physical appearances on the front lines, were almost over. She had reluctantly given up her "Six Trips Afield" in 1964 on the eve of her seventy-ninth birthday. It was estimated that some 15,000 students had followed this inspiring teacher during the forty-five consecutive years of these trips, often braving the roughest weather the bay area could offer, along bay shores, through city parks, and botanic gardens, woodlands, and chaparral, and over the wildflower strewn ridges in the spring. Through all these years she had missed ten classes.

Junea Kelly's last public appearance that I remember was for the dedication in November 1967 of the Junea W. Kelly Garden for the Birds in the Strybing Arboretum in Golden Gate Park. It required devoted friends and a wheelchair to get her there. Of all the man-made habitats of the bay area, this arboretum was a most favored place; perhaps she left her heart there. I like to seek out the bench dedicated to her in a hidden corner of the native garden and recall the words borrowed from Harold Gilliam at the close of that ceremony: "Her eyes have seen the Glory of the wonders of creation." A friend added, "And she has shared this Glory with thousands."

She Saved Seashores
and Sanctuaries:
Laurel Reynolds

LAUREL REYNOLDS, whose wildlife films were to entertain and inform scores of thousands, save seashores and wildlife sanctuaries, even move Congress, was not a born naturalist. Very pretty, somewhat shy, and a star student, her proclivities were literary, and she had a secret yen to become a dancer. Her marriage to Eric Reynolds shaped her life and her career, providing the role which she fulfilled so brilliantly.

Laurel and Eric met in Los Angeles during World War I when he was an ensign in the Navy. The only son of an English gentleman farmer in Washington state, he grew up with a passion for birds and mammals and other wild things. He displayed an insatiable curiosity toward their lives.

They married against the opposition of Ric's mother. He had entertained ambitions of becoming a professional naturalist, but the responsibilities of marriage changed his mind. Medicine became his new goal. Laurel, who had worked as a secretary to help support her family, now worked to help her husband through medical school.

The natural world claimed the leisure time of the young Dr. Reynolds. He and Laurel regularly took the ferry from San Francisco to Marin County and the little train up Mount Tamalpais to hike and to bird.

A son, a daughter, and an automobile were added to the family. The Sunday excursions continued and expanded, hiking up other mountain slopes, tramping through insect-ridden marshes and clambering over slippery rocks to observe shore birds—all to add to Ric's life list of birds.

Laurel, by then not so slender and athletic, didn't always share this enthusiasm of father and children and often complained. "I'm spoiling your pleasure, isn't that true?" she would ask her husband. "Well, yes you are," he'd admit gently, while racking his brains to come up with a solution that would keep them together out-of-doors as a family.

Doctor Ric found the solution—a motion picture camera for Laurel! Gradually the Sunday excursions became photographic expeditions with father discovering the subjects and the children dutifully toting tripod, lenses, and spare film to location. Domestic harmony was restored. During those early years Laurel built up an invaluable record of California wildlife: sandhill cranes nesting in Modoc county, brown pelicans loafing and posing at Point Lobos, bushtits and hummingbirds building nests in the Reynolds garden.

World War II suddenly changed all that. As a doctor in the Navy Medical Reserve, Ric was immediately dispatched to the South Pacific Theater where he soon distinguished himself in the combat zones and eventually became chief surgeon. The children went off to boarding schools. Laurel, left alone, became an avid filmmaker. She studied photography and editing at evening schools and converted a bedroom into a workshop with desk, files, and editing equipment. She remade her first films of wildlife in their Piedmont garden into a more professional film.

A premiere showing of *Fun With Birds* at the 1939 World's Fair on Treasure Island may have convinced Laurel and Ric that she should someday go pro. She had already responded to a number of invitations to show this film—and that was only the beginning. She produced eleven films in thirty years, lectured for the National Audubon Society for seventeen years, showed films at the festival presentations of the American Museum of Natural History in New York, became a Chataqua lecturer, and delighted and inspired audiences at schools, universities, and clubs. Among her honors and awards was a bronze medal from the Audubon Society. Somewhere along the way, shy Laurel had changed into a real pro.

The Reynolds' Piedmont garden, the never-failing source of subjects and inspiration for Laurel, was like an out-of-door movie set with live characters. The gray trunks of live oaks towered over groups of ferns, rhododendrons, and azaleas. Dense thickets provided cover for ground-dwelling birds, and there was an irregularly-shaped pond with shallow pools for drinking and bathing. An early breakfast of bird seeds and cracked corn was served on carefully positioned trays, and before dinner time, corn was scattered on the lawn to lure quail families from adjacent, wilder land. In fall and winter large flocks of band-tailed pigeons swooped in to crowd lesser birds from feeding trays, and a brush rabbit frequently ventured out from cover for the corn on the lawn. Jays kept up incessant, inconclusive arguments.

Every spring bushtits returned to build their elongated nests in the great spreading oak by the front door, secluded by a rose-lined driveway from the street. Hummingbirds flashed back and forth from fuschias and other nectar sources to sip sugared water from feeders hung along the patio. In the fall, there were abundant red berries on toyon and pyracantha for the hosts of cedar waxwings and robins, while the few resident robins also found worms on the rich lawn.

A garden like that doesn't just happen. Before she began her film adventures with birds in the garden, Laurel often resented the endless hours of weeding, watering, pruning, replanting, and other chores. Head gardener Ric had insisted that the entire family share this work. Many years later, overlooking the shaggy fruit trees and wild blackberry and cow parsnip at her daughter's home, Laurel sighed and said, "I love your garden." Ariel, her daughter, remembering the lovely Piedmont garden, asked why. "It's so restful," answered her mother. "It looks as if nobody ever did anything to it."

Security for the Reynolds garden birds had required vigorous measures. Abandoned cats dropped off along Dimond Canyon below their property were a greater threat than that offered by all the native predators, bird, mammalian, and reptilian combined.

One early morning I called at the Reynolds home to find the doctor coming from the outer edges of his property with a small bore rifle and a shovel. "I don't enjoy doing this, Paul," he confessed, "but the ecology of this place has to be kept in balance by some big predator like me. Laurel had her camera focused on a feeding tray when a stalking cat came into the frame. Nesting quail and towhees are no match for those cats."

On the more positive side was the hospice for orphaned and injured birds and mammals that demanded so much household time—and the doctor's frequent medical skills. A large outdoor cage was usually occupied by some avian guest, ranging from the distinguished to the humble. It might be a horned owl, kestrel, or raven, with other cages for a skunk, a gopher, or little kangaroo rats. Once a brood of Canada geese grew up in the garden, and when adult were taken to distant Puget Sound for release. When father found and brought home the injured or orphan subject, the children were drafted as nurses, and mother took stunning close-ups of it all. For many years the Reynolds' sympathetic, cultured housekeeper, Misaye Wetemale, served as assistant supervisor of this menagerie. On one occasion her successful care and rearing of an orphan robin became a Laurel wild-bird narrative.

The highpoint in all those years of bird rearing, either by the natural parents or the Reynolds' hospice, was the wood duck episode of 1941. The female of a pair in residence began behaving strangely. Her wings were not clipped like her mate's, and she flew off to harass the goldfish in a neighbor's pond, then returned to explore every recess in the garden.

Wood ducks nest in cavities of old trees, the books state, so Doctor Ric found and wired several sections of rotting logs with cavities to trees in strategic sites. Mrs. Woody, with her white-spectacled eyes, investigated them one by one and rejected them all. Laurel's brother-in-law, not a naturalist but an engineer, insisted on building a geometrically perfect plywood box with a large hole and placed it in a cotoneaster bush some thirty inches above the pond.

Imagine the mixed chagrin and joy in the Reynolds house-hold when they watched Mrs. Woody move into the man-made manor, lay a clutch of eggs, and settle down to incubate! She proved to be a good mother, and within a few weeks a brood of grayish fluffy ducklings were bobbing on the pond.

As a busy general practitioner and surgeon, Doctor Ric never had enough time for the natural world. His great heart and empathy with the aging as well as the ill involved him in the growing social problems. He later became president of the California Medical Association and of the California Physicians Service (later known as Blue Shield). He also worked with the state on the setup of the medical plan. But each working morning he would remind Laurel of a nest or other subject she planned to photograph and later inquired about the details. And many evenings were devoted to his growing ornithological library. His powers of retention from reading and observation were extraordinary. Roger Tory Peterson, the noted ornithologist, once remarked: "Ric knows more shore birds than any man in North America."

Though Laurel might disdain some details of zoology and botany, she became an expert in the biological processes of family life—both human and animal. She loved children. She understood play, affection, sex, marital squabbles, and domestic responsibility. Whether it was the courtship problems of the phalarope or the shared feeding of young pileated woodpeckers, she could describe it accurately and amusingly. Audiences loved her and, through her, her subjects. To find favor simultaneously with learned professors of ornithology, sophisticated club women, and restless elementary school classes was indeed an impressive accomplishment. It marked a successful educator combined with an entertainer.

A remarkable talent for effective communication and diplomacy was demonstrated by Laurel's constant and voluminous correspondence, much of it related to her screen tour schedules and invitations she couldn't fill. Daughter Ariel recalls that she once suggested that she and her mother should discuss controversial matters by mail for quicker, smoother solutions.

High adventure and brushes with disaster became commonplace for wildlife photographer Reynolds. Was it her quick reflexes, determination, a handy friend, or a guardian angel that saved her from death or serious injury at those times?

Despite driving thousands of miles yearly, Laurel had never quite mastered the automobile. While rushing from a performance many miles away to attend her son Gordon's wedding in Palo Alto she managed to stall her car on the tracks of the Southern Pacific commuter railroad—just as the gates descended and bells clanged.

"Lady, lady, get out quick!" yelled a policeman who suddenly appeared. The locomotive was now bearing down, horn blasting and brakes grinding.

"Just a minute. I have to get my camera and stuff out!" called back Laurel, tugging at two large packages in the seat beside her. "My films are in the trunk!"

The officer didn't wait for more protestations, but grabbed her car door and yanked. Out came Laurel towing her camera and screaming, "My film is in the trunk!" A few seconds later she was standing by the gates viewing the remains of her yellow car. The monster locomotive loomed over it. Just then members of the family who had turned back found her there, one shoe off and one shoe on, unscratched. The films too somehow escaped damage.

World War II brought unforeseen risks for wildlife watchers and photographers, even around San Francisco Bay. One day Laurel took along Misaye to help her film caspian terns at their nesting colony on a levee north of the Dumbarton bridge. They were unaware that this was a military off-limits zone. Laurel and Misaye were promptly spotted and arrested by the Coast Guard. Released on bail, they promised never again to spy on the United States government!

Even wildlife filming at the Lake Merritt Waterfowl Refuge could be hazardous. I as park naturalist had rowed Laurel to one of the duck islands to record the nesting of a pair of mute swans. Just as she got set up and focused, the male charged. Under those powerful flailing wings, Laurel, tripod, camera, and swan would soon have merged in a heap. I simply thrust out the wire rake I carried at such times and interrupted the charge. The filming continued.

There were many other incidents, such as the time she nearly fell off the cliff at Point Reyes while attempting to approach more closely the beached sea lions, and again when she almost capsized a boat in Mexico in the excitement of a whale breaching right alongside.

By the 1950s many of the outstanding natural resources of the San Francisco bay area were in real jeopardy. A review of Laurel Reynolds' films reveals that she photographed these wonders of nature, and these areas have been saved partly as a direct result of her splendid and convincing films.

Audubon Canyon Ranch* over at Bolinas Bay in Marin Coun-

* Audubon Canyon Ranch is normally open to the public on weekends from March to early July. Address inquiries to Audubon Canyon Ranch, 4900 Highway One, Stinson Beach, CA 94920. Teachers should inquire regarding scheduling classes at the adjacent Volunteer Canyon, where overnight stays are possible.

Laurel Reynolds with portable blind (Mindy Willis photo).

ty is one such example. Laurel and Ric were active members of the Golden Gate chapter of the National Audubon Society. The Golden Gate chapter, together with the Marin and Sequoia (San Francisco peninsula) chapters, were engaged in a desperate effort to acquire a small farm and a large grove of redwoods which supported a nesting colony of great egrets and great blue herons. The adjacent tideflats of Bolinas Bay yielded abundant food for their young in spring. The property also included a small fresh-water marsh and trails winding uphill through forest to coastal scrub and grassland. This was far too precious to become future housing!

Laurel agreed to make a film for this cause for the cost of film and processing. The private lives of these striking birds on and around the treetop nest platforms could be filmed by telescopic lens from a hillside lookout at a level slightly above them. Courtship display and nest building began in March. Three months later most of the fledglings were ready to take off, though some late starts and setbacks often prolonged the season into July. This meant many, many trips at frequent intervals up a steep path loaded with heavy photographic equipment.

With characteristic determination Laurel maintained the self-imposed schedule of trips to Bolinas Bay to record the entire nesting cycle. *Audubon Canyon Ranch* played to full houses of schools, clubs, and environmental groups around the bay area. With this invaluable boost, purchase of the original property was completed in 1961. Later, large tracts of adjoining properties were added.

Jutting out into the Pacific, Point Reyes peninsula in Marin County remained a land of broad beaches, dense forest tracts and large dairy farms even after World War II. Except for the ranchers, the road to the lighthouse, and some secluded coves popular with bathers, Point Reyes hadn't changed much since the times of explorers Drake and Cermeno, the traders, and the whalers. Of course the Indian occupants had vanished. A few residential lots had been sold at Limantour Spit, an area noted for its dune flora and archeological remains and wintering waterfowl. This was enough to trigger an alarm among environmentalists and de-votees of this unspoiled coast. Logging projects had started in the forest along Bolinas Ridge. To cap it all, developers were lobbying for a wide commuter highway to replace the tortuous cliffside road from Mill Valley to Stinson Beach, Bolinas, and this ridge area. "You can sleep by the ocean at Drake's Lagoon and be at your San Francisco office thirty minutes later," they promised. Fighting words, those!

The National Park Service unexpectedly entered the picture in 1958. A 1935 survey and proposal to acquire Point Reyes was hurriedly dusted off, printed and distributed to key legislators. Congressman Clem Miller from Marin and Senator Clair Engle spearheaded the drive in Washington; Senator Peter Behr of Marin and other key legislators plugged it in Sacramento. The Sierra Club became a focus for local action on Point Reyes.

Some convincing film propaganda was urgently needed. A blue ribbon committee asked Laurel Reynolds if she would consider filming Point Reyes. She accepted the challenge. For years Laurel had been recording Point Reyes wildlife, flora, and landscapes. Now she set out to supplement, delete, combine and edit. The noted environmental writer Harold Gilliam came up with the perfect title for her finished film: *Island in Time*. Today, after hundreds of showings, this film still is in demand. It is a dazzling sequence of breathtaking seascapes, flower-studded slopes and meadows, nesting murres and quarreling sea lions, children poking into tidepools, and even courting bullfrogs in a pond.

The opposition to a Point Reyes National Seashore soon mustered its forces. Developers continued to get building permits from the Marin County board of supervisors. Most of the ranchers just wanted to be left alone. Members of several hunting club preserves brought political pressure to bear. Few pro-park people sympathized with the developers or sportsmen, but some felt sorry for the ranchers. To make matters worse, the Eisenhower administration just couldn't see appropriating monies for another national park at that time.

Never giving up, Congressman Miller arranged for the proper congressional committees to view *Island in Time*. Citizen names by the thousands and an impressive list of organizational petitions had already reached their offices.

After the inauguration of President John F. Kennedy, there was an abrupt change of attitude in Washington. New Interior Secretary Stewart Udall talked and acted like an environmentalist. There was a precedent in an existing national seashore where the old-time residents and farmers coexisted with a public park— Cape Cod National Seashore in Massachusetts. This plan applied to Point Reyes. Congress passed the Point Reyes National

Seashore bill in August of 1962 and President Kennedy signed it on September 15. The bill called for 53,600 acres but appropriated only $13 million for purchases.

This inadequate appropriation proved lamentable and short-sighted. Less than half of the seashore had been purchased before the Nixon administration in 1969 suspended all park acquisitions in an economy drive. This created an awkward situation at Point Reyes. While most bay area people thought they had their seashore, those who patronized it knew better. Some new homes were appearing; key access roads bore No Trespassing signs. Some new action was demanded or the people would be cheated.

It often takes just one incident to set off a wide alarm. On this occasion Laurel and Ric had taken John Baker, the stately president of National Audubon, out to Limantour Lagoon for a weekend picnic. Havoc greeted them on the little access road over the hills. Bulldozers had just cut a wide geometric swath. Three of the monsters were sitting there waiting to resume their orgy of destruction on Monday!

A new call to arms soon spread throughout the bay area, across northern California, and then back to New York and Washington with John Baker. The Sierra Club distributed copies of *Island in Time* to scores of school assemblies, garden and service clubs, city councils, and county supervisors' meetings. A new deluge of letters and phone calls descended on Congress—even an appeal from California's Republican-dominated Assembly. It was more than President Nixon and his administration could withstand. It was agreed that the seashore would be completed. The amount eventually spent totalled $56 million. Delay had been very costly.

Laurel Reynolds always found time for lesser causes and more modest projects for the public welfare near home. Such was the appeal of Oakland Parks Superintendent William Penn Mott, Jr., for a film-showing to help with fund-raising for a visitors center at the Lake Merritt Waterfowl Refuge. The park naturalist program needed a home and information center.

Laurel and Ric had watched this program develop and wanted to help. A showing of *Western Discovery* was scheduled for the Oakland Auditorium Theater. The sum raised added a nice increment to the building fund and the Rotary Natural Science Center was opened in September 1953. As park naturalist I was a principal beneficiary.

Two decades as a National Audubon wildlife lecturer and acceptance by a national booking agency kept Laurel traveling the circuit across the country part of each year. Husband Ric then had the household, his garden, and birds, as well as his practice to handle. Her grown children sometimes questioned whether all of her absences were really essential and fully rewarding. Then Ariel and her husband recalled the banquet back in the 1940s.

This California woman, Laurel Reynolds, would be the first woman ever to address a National Audubon Society annual banquet. Ariel and her husband were then living in New England and had been invited to attend. They still remember the Park Avenue mansion where Laurel was hosted, the limousine ride with mink lap robes, and Audubon president, John Baker, introducing guest Reynolds with his Back Bay accent. Laurel was a fashion plate in her Christian Dior gown.

The Audubon wildlife lecturers were indeed a distinguished company, including such names as Carl Bucheister (later Audubon president), Dr. Ernest P. Edwards, Eban McMillan, Karl Maslowski, Robert Hernes, and Colin Fletcher.

All these great naturalists appeared in the bay area at various times and were usually guests at the Reynolds' Piedmont home, often accompanied by their supportive wives. Many of the local Audubonites came to boast acquaintance with them. Laurel and Ric were gracious hosts, but the guests' demands for transportation here and there must have sometimes become strenuous. Only once did I hear a complaint from Doctor Ric. That was the time a screen tour lecturer, his wife, and their large boisterous dog arrived by auto. For the sake of the garden and the wildlife inhabitants they were "permitted to sleep elsewhere"!

The Reynolds hosted an annual garden party for the Golden Gate Audubon Society. It was staged when the rhododendrons, azaleas, and fuchsias were in full bloom, and there was constant bird song and activity. A favorite after-dinner entertainer was Bert Harwell, renowned Yosemite naturalist, with his bird songs and whistles. Even the local birds were temporarily hushed. Later, during one question period, a boy piped up to ask what kind of birdseed Mr. Harwell ate for breakfast. When darkness fell one of Laurel's films was always shown.

Since the hosts had provided so much, the society's treasurer was able to report a tidy profit from the hundred or more guest reservations. This event was a fundraiser to boost the scholarship fund that sent selected teachers, young ranger-naturalists, and other outdoor educators to the Audubon Camp of California (later closed in favor of an Audubon Camp of the West in Wyoming).

The likely casualties of this annual affair could have been the hosts and their invaluable Misaye, who had actually cooked the food as well! In 1959, when it finally was decided to call in a caterer to feed 200 guests, Laurel spoke of their decision as "the liberation."

Next to Laurel's own family and Misaye, Mindy Willis was unquestionably the greatest reward in human form that ever came Laurel's way. Mindy, a niece of Herbert Hoover, married a professor's son, Neal Willis, who turned his father's geological knowledge to good account in the oil business. Neal and Mindy lingered after the audience departed at a Los Angeles showing of a Reynolds film. Mindy knew motion picture photography, pursued nature subjects, and had endless patience. That encounter late in the 1950s began a friendship and partnership that produced five films and resulted in photographic expeditions up and down California and to Mexico, Alaska and Africa!

The teamwork of Reynolds-Willis was admirable and perhaps a rare example. Laurel remained editor-in-chief. She did the narrations when sound was added; that took a bit of ham and rapport with every type of audience. Mindy specialized in time-lapse photography. In the field both partners might be seen with cameras trained simultaneously on the same subject. Even more editing was then required.

High adventure mixed with pure relaxation resulted when the two couples could get together for discovery and filming with the *Thundercloud*, the eighty-seven foot yacht owned by the Willises. Such experiences occurred on one Baja California trip whose log Mindy thoughtfully loaned for this account. Their Mexican ventures had contributed to two films: *Mexico's California* and *New World Rediscovered*.

San Ignacio Lagoon on the lower west coast of Baja California was far more primitive and peaceful when the Willis-Reynolds team explored it compared to the winter seasons of later years. A procession of whale-watching boats, research teams, and even helicopter-borne observer-photographers, have greatly altered the scenes these friends enjoyed.

In one film, narrator Ric commented: "On the boat and on the beach, one is seldom out of earshot of the sound they (the gray whales) make when exhaling. A curious sound it is, reminiscent of the thrilling noise of childhood—of steam locomotives as they idled at their depot stops."

This narrative was cut short by a whale breaching near the *Thundercloud*. Continued Ric, "Almost two-thirds of the great mammal appeared before it flopped back into the lagoon. Yesterday there was a female who seemed to have two young—right beside the boat. In fact, Neal became acquainted with the mother and began calling her two children Ike and Mike. . . ."

Cabo San Lucas, extreme southern tip of Baja, was relatively unspoiled when the *Thundercloud* dropped anchor. A rented car enabled the discoverers to visit several remote beaches and tiny villages. Laurel and Mindy filmed schoolchildren and commented on their friendliness. Birdlife-listers would drool at the mention of many of their bird photo scoops, like the Xanthus hummingbird, San Lucas sharp-winged nighthawk, and San Lucas thrasher.

The lure of big fish jumping all about the *Thundercloud* was irresistible. Both couples joined the crew with rods and reels. Large dolphins (the fish and not the mammal), bonita, and Pacific mackerel came aboard daily. Enough fish and lobsters for a party feast could be bought on shore for a few pesos, or even a carton of cigarettes if one were a trader. Little did these and other *norteamericano* visitors of that era realize that their pictorial proofs of this paradise would bring hordes of fisherfolks and tourists—even a "jet set"—to Cabo San Lucas a few years later.

Long files of brown pelicans and boobies crossed ahead or astern of the *Thundercloud* when it sailed the Sea of Cortez (the Gulf of Baja). Frigate birds soared overhead until they spotted a pelican or other fisherman with a catch they could plunder in a lightning dive. Whales of several species surfaced, spouted or breached around them, while porpoise streaked ahead just under the forepeak. One night Laurel dreamed that the *Thundercloud* was hoisted on the back of a huge whale and spun about!

Laurel wrote of landing on tiny Santa Isabel Island in the gulf: "I felt that I'd found a new botanical world because the bushes, though of normal size, bore enormous, globular red fruits. It suggested the grandstand at a football game with everyone dressed in green and holding a large red balloon. This effect was caused by hundreds of male frigate birds, sitting on their carelessly assembled nests, extending their pouches of red skin beneath their bills. We think the male builds the nest and then tries to attract the females."

Doctor Ric summed up the advantages of birding in Baja and elsewhere on the west coast of Mexico in his scholarly way: "The combination of sea, desert, mountains, and tropical jungle conspire to add species and varieties of avifauna much greater than that of all North America above the border put together. Also, because of the hourglass position of Mexico between the two continents and with its offshore islands, it is a likely place for vagrants and stragglers."

Ariel relates with a chuckle how the two husbands, Doctor Ric and Neal the oilman, would get into heated political arguments. Reynolds was a Democrat and humanitarian with some pro-socialist leanings, while Willis preached the advantages of capitalism and Republicanism. Social conflict might have ended more than one happy productive cruise but for the pacifying ministrations of Laurel and Mindy in the privacy of their respective cabins.

Laurel and Mindy and their camera eyes would once again join a major political battle early in the 1960s. San Francisco Bay itself and its connecting estuaries were in mortal peril. In little over a century only some sixty square miles of saltmarsh remained of the original 600 square miles. The rest had been reclaimed for agriculture and various uses, or converted by diking to salt ponds. Municipalities filling for expansion, private developers, sport boating and shipping interests had been responsible. Now a new demand on remaining marsh and tideflat was mounting. "It's the logical place for the garbage or solid waste dump," announced local planners and politicians. "Just see what we'll have when it's leveled off in ten years: a subdivision on the bay with room for a golf course and a public park too!"

"The bay as we know it will depart into history, as surely as did the bay that Portola discovered and Father Font described with awe," wrote Mel Scott in his study of the time. Scott's vision of "parks and shoreline drives, new ports, and well-ordered industries" was shared by a growing number of citizens and groups. But governors, legislatures, the newly formed Association of Bay Area Governments (ABAG), and federal agencies such as the Army Corps of Engineers had failed to get any strong protective action. A San Francisco Bay Conservation and Development Commission (BCDC) was a concept being urged by many environmentalists. Such a body would control all filling and building permits within a prescribed distance of deep water or mean high tide line.

Harold Gilliam in his 1957 book *San Francisco Bay* had written: "For most of the bay to be replaced by mile after mile of solidly built-up suburbs would be to eliminate the area's greatest natural advantage." As a San Francisco *Chronicle* feature writer he was able to keep expounding on the vanishing bay crisis and stimulate other media and citizen efforts. Bold citizenship was crucial. Who would pick up the standard?

Three Berkeley women, Esther Gulick, Kay Kerr, and Sylvia McLaughlin met at Sylvia's home one memorable day in 1961. They had invited a senator, an engineer, a biologist, and a planner—each to discuss his views and proposals on bay problems. Notes were carefully kept.

More meetings followed with more experts giving input. Mrs. Morse Erskine of San Francisco and Dr. Will Siri joined the nucleus. Graphic information leaflets were printed and widely distributed with invitations to send in a dollar and join the Save San Francisco Bay Association. Scores joined at once, then hundreds, then thousands. William Penn Mott, Jr., then general manager of the East Bay Regional Parks, became association president.

Mindy Willis and Laurel Reynolds in action (Mindy Willis photo).

Doctor Ric and Laurel naturally became involved in this new environmental groundswell. "These women have turned everyone in the bay area into a conservationist," remarked Ric. But he couldn't have meant this literally. Opposition to any new agency or form of governmental control was strong, with the usual lobbying pressures exerted on decision makers, from city councils to county supervisors to the legislature. Clearly, a mass education effort was needed to move citizens to exert pressure to save the bay.

Laurel Reynolds and her partner Mindy Willis were ready and willing to assist this cause. They were commissioned to produce a film to (1) present the desperate need and the proposed solutions; (2) persuade the thousands who would view the film; and (3) demand positive action.

When Laurel and Mindy set out to chronicle the bay, only a few miles of beaches and shore were open to the public. This female film team became a familiar sight around the bay at sports marinas, public fishing piers, or alongside a crowded party fishing boat. But there were other sites "off-limits" to the public that also demanded recording, such as garbage dumps swarming with gulls, and new landfills. So these normally law-abiding women barged in with their cameras and got into trouble.

"You saw the signs but came in just the same. Now you'll stay here until I get the deputies," one landfill operator in effect told them. But he yielded to persuasion and released them. Another developer chased them off and threatened to confiscate their film.

The thousands of migrant shorebirds populating the sandy beaches and tideflats of Alameda had attracted many wildlife photographers. The spectacle of these vast flocks rising, wheeling, executing serial maneuvers, and suddenly settling against a sunset was considered the climax of this Laurel-Mindy film (Walt Disney later asked them for similar footage). Laurel appropriately called this part "The Living Sands of San Francisco Bay." Could we afford to destroy the wintering place of these migrants? Could we deny posterity the opportunity to enjoy such scenes?

Time was rapidly running out for many of these natural events pictured by Laurel and Mindy. Salt marshes and tidelands were still regarded as wastelands by many local politicians and planners. A handful of biologists were trying to demonstrate that, besides supporting many species of shore, water, and wading birds of the Pacific Flyway, the marshes were nurseries for the sportfish and shellfish of the bay, while the mudflats purified the waters that lapped across them twice daily.

The moving film *San Francisco Bay* was completed and released in 1966. In addition to the plant and animal life, it handsomely documented the purely human uses of the bay—sailing, fishing, beachcombing, dipping, and swimming. Among its many viewers in northern California were sympathetic but procrastinating citizens who had long seen the need but failed to act. Now they picked up telephones or paper and pens and deluged the state legislature and Congress with their demands. Under the leadership of State Senators Nicholas Petris, Peter Behr, Howard Way, and others, a San Francisco Bay Development and Conservation bill was passed at Sacramento and signed by the governor. Laurel and Mindy, their friends, and co-workers were justly proud.

But three years after the advent of the BCDC (and even to this day) much of San Francisco Bay's shores remained in jeopardy. Harold Gilliam recognized this in 1969 when he wrote the book entitled *Between the Devil and the Deep Blue Bay*. In the few years that had passed since his first volume on the bay, he noted that more than an additional ten square miles were reclaimed.

The Corps of Engineers had warned that if filling and diking continued at this rate the bay would be reduced to a channel within 100 years. Gilliam's chapters titled "A Billion Years at Bay Farm Island" and "On the Pacific Flyway" are loaded with factual information bay protectors could fire at their opponents. About the Laurel-Mindy film he wrote, "As the first film on the subject . . . *San Francisco Bay* played a vital role in focusing public opinion on this environmental movement."

"What makes you think you can make a film?" Laurel with a smile asked her daughter Ariel one day in the 1970s. Though a painter and designer by profession, Ariel had found time for environmental activities that won her a grant from the Environmental Protection Agency to make a film on waste management.

With characteristic self-confidence and the camera techniques she had quietly picked up, Ariel went ahead on her film *Use It, Use It Up*. Mother of course made her film footage library available, and many shots of the Bay Farm Island fills were used. Two photographer friends, Scott and Anderson, worked on the editing. With some of Laurel's closeup studies, from mushrooms to insects to hummingbirds and sapsuckers, Ariel was able to show that recycling is the rule of nature, not the exception.

The film *Use It, Use It Up* premiered at the Academy of Sciences in Golden Gate Park and later won an award at the American Film Festival. A joint triumph for Ariel and Laurel, it was Laurel's last professional effort.

A secluded cove on the Hood Canal in the Evergreen Empire of Washington state became the retirement home of Laurel and Doctor Ric. "Canal" is misleading—the whole environment with its towering Olympics suggests a Norwegian fjord. Many years before they had purchased this property on Guillemot Cove. Her popular film *Magic Basket* had been made there, with her two-year-old granddaughter in the principal role.

Ric gave up his fifty-year-old medical practice. The Piedmont home was sold to finance the building of a made-to-order house at the cove. A little cupola or sunroom atop the house might be used to watch birds on the cove or to spot farmer Ric in his spacious garden. For this was the garden, surrounded by evergreen forest and bird voices that he must have often envisioned when medical and administrative problems and hectic weekly schedules bore heavily on him.

One never-to-be-forgotten day in the course of a northwest vacation trip, four of us longtime friends of the Reynolds family found our way to Guillemot Cove at the end of a narrow forest road twelve miles from the nearest village. We had phoned ahead to alert the Reynolds and receive driving instructions.

"Oh, Ric's somewhere out there in the garden," Laurel said a little dryly after greeting us and showing us around their modern functional home. She agreed to ride along as a guide and continue the visit as we ate our picnic lunch.

A man with a hoe in the midst of a luxuriant vegetable garden was soon recognized as the object of our search. Proudly Doctor Ric showed off his towering bean stalks, glossy corn, and intricate lettuces that thrived in the rich alluvial soil. When we complimented him on his achievements, he smiled and observed that the deer and rabbits liked it too.

At the children's cottage or beach house just beyond we spent an hour reminiscing, recalling birding and film adventures, and many Audubon friends. Ric seemed quite content here, but Laurel hadn't quite adapted to rural life. Fortunately son Gordon and family lived in the Puget Sound area and Ariel visited frequently.

A male housekeeper and kitchen hand by the name of Melvin

Laurel Reynolds and Roger Tory Peterson at Lake Merritt..

was a find for the Reynolds. He became indispensable to the household operation when family and friends arrived to stay over.

But one day Ric assumed the role of master of both house and estate and whisked poor Melvin away to a trail-clearing project he considered a high priority before Melvin could even clear the breakfast table.

A great clatter arose from the house as iron pots, platters, and lids went hurtling across the porch and onto the landscape. Laurel emerged with two suitcases, marched to her car, and took off up the road. She was later located in a motel halfway to Bremerton, busying herself with some film editing. Melvin was not seen at the cove after that event.

Ric and Laurel were eventually obliged to give up life at Guillemot Cove and move to a comfortable retirement apartment in Berkeley. Here there was another garden where Doctor Ric's ministrations were most welcome. His last moments on this earth were spent pulling weeds in that garden.

In the early 1980s a picture and social evening for Laurel was

held in Berkeley by Ariel and friends. I was privileged to participate as the projectionist. After we had viewed *The Magic Basket*
and another film made by Laurel, she rose to recall some of the
circumstances that led her to make these and other films.

Ariel remembers a conversation thirty years ago between
Laurel and the anthropologist Gertrude Toffelmier. They were
playing a game. "If you could choose one gift or power, what
would it be?" Gertrude, in a velvet dress, her white-blond hair
waved back from her temples, her brown eyes large and well-
shaped as a doe's, said, "Beauty." Laurel said, "I would want to
handle well every situation life gave to me."

Botanist of Del Norte:
Ruby Steele Van Deventer

A SUMMER NATURE-TRAINING camp in the high Sierra of California is sure to be a rich and unforgettable experience for any chosen group of adults or youngsters. The Audubon Camp of California, held in the 1950s at the Sugar Bowl, just below Donner Pass in the Sierra Nevada, was among the most prestigious and rewarding of all such opportunities in western United States. At each two-week session the staff consisted of experienced professional instructors and the students were teachers, camp counselors, ranger-naturalists, or dedicated Audubon volunteers. Many of these students had been screened and chosen for scholarships by local Audubon chapters.

Almost everything that grew, crawled, swam, left tracks, flew, or uttered a call or song in that vibrant summer environment could be identified by one or another of the staff. Even those lovely mute rocks and clouds that gathered overhead each afternoon had their skilled interpreters. A popular mammalogist, Dr. Ferd Ruth, attracted both admiration and much humorous comment about his interpretation of mammal scats (excreta) as well as footprints. "Doctor of Scatology," they dubbed him, and even made up a ditty about him for the final social gathering!

Then there was Ruby. Ruby Van Deventer from Fort Dick in Del Norte County, California. A rather heavyset, middle-aged woman with plain features, she might have passed for just another school teacher or dedicated nature buff—except for a personality that made instant friends, reinforced self-esteem and purpose, and frequently imparted a bit of relevant, supplemental information on the subject of the moment.

It was upon the granite ledges at Donner Pass that Ruby had her big moment in the sun. The occasion was a combined geology and natural history study excursion which meant some fifty students and most of the staff. The leader told about the origin of this northern Sierra uplift, the exposure and exfoliation of the granites, had them listen to nutcrackers' raucous voices off in the stunted pines, and then—

Ruby was out in front of the class with the ready assent of the staff. "Friends," she announced loud and clear, "we should remember the 49ers and the later pioneers who struggled up and over this pass with their covered wagons. My grandparents were among them in 1852, so I've heard the story from some who did it. Once I thought I'd found the marks of those wagon wheels on the granite over there. But down in Emigrant Gap I could show you where those wagons were lowered on ropes over a cliff, even taken down and put together at the bottom. My folks fared better than the Donner Party who arrived out there east of this divide in early winter."

Ruby became indispensable to those of us who were indulging our botanic pursuits, even if we had registered for the mammal class. Audubon's summer course wisely combined all interest groups on some field trips. Everywhere the bright-hued high Sierra and alpine flowers demanded attention, from those in lush meadows to the dainty species tucked in among the granite ledges. Several students could recognize most of them, but Ruby knew virtually every species. And since the staff botanist had come from southern California, Ruby found herself the guest botanist giving the answers.

For those who lingered with her at the dinner table or around the fireplace after evening programs, Ruby revealed fascinating accounts of pioneer history and of the Indians of Del Norte and Humboldt she had come to know and love. No staff member or other camper could match such first-hand experiences.

Invitations to visit Ruby and her husband at their Smith River home were rewards for a few of us who listened and questioned this pioneer teacher. "The old homestead has extra bedrooms and cots; bring your spouses and children, too," Ruby added with utmost sincerity.

Ruby was born in 1892 on the north bank of the Smith River, one of four children of the Steele family, themselves children of pioneers. Her other playmates were mostly Tolowa Indians from the reservation across the river. How to spear fish, swim in turbulent waters, build a campfire, and shoot straight were among ways learned from these Indians. A 3½ mile walk to school exposed Ruby to many fascinating plants and some wildlife. A family biographer later compared her with two other famed California botanists who became botanical collectors, Lester Rowantree of Carmel and Edith Van Allen Murphy of Covelo.

High school at Crescent City, where she would later teach foreign languages for twenty-two years, was Ruby's next goal. Though her father scorned such higher education for a girl, she earned room and board with a local family and commuted home weekends by logging train.

Ruby's next academic target was the University of California at Berkeley. Her mother had died and left her some timber rights for this express purpose. Ruby still had to work at both the library and infirmary to help pay her way. Holiday visits to her father and the old homestead frequently entailed dangerous voyages by coastal lumber steamers. Many times during a raging storm and high seas she rode ashore or back to ship in a "bosun's britches"— a rope life line from one to the other.

The golden blond hair, striking features, and vivacious manner of co-ed Steele caught the attention of President Theodore "Teddy" Roosevelt when he came to lecture at the university. Ruby spoke to him and then escorted him across the campus from the Greek Theater after his first lecture; that became a daily occurrence for the remainder of the President's stay. We wonder if she invited him to the Smith River country for elk or bear hunting.

A teaching job in the Mohave Desert lured Ruby away from the university after her first year. At the end of the school year she

took some of her earnings for a trip by fruit steamer to Mexico. She
and some fellow passengers planned to return by rail, but the
revolutionists of 1912 changed that by ripping up tracks. So the
party bargained for mules and guides and rode in a more leisurely
manner back to the U. S. border.

Graduation from the university remained Ruby's immediate
goal. She returned to Berkeley and by staying through summer
school finished in another two years. She refused the teaching
position offered at Los Angeles and returned to the north woods.

Ruby met young Arthur Van Deventer while visiting the
Oregon lumber town of Brookings. "I knew immediately that he
was the right man," she would confide later. They were married
within days. Soon Van, as she affectionately called him, became
district ranger for the Siskiyou National Forest and the two made
their home in this roadless wilderness. Ruby could hunt, fish, and
study the flora to her heart's content. Only the birth of daughter
Dwayne in 1920 led them to settle in the family homestead on
Smith River.

The magic name Smith River alone is enough to set many an
outdoor-minded Californian checking his highway maps and
camping, fishing, or photography gear. The Smith is the last major
undammed river of California and drains a huge watershed that
remains close to wilderness, except for logging operations and
scattered mines and farms.

Here is a quote from a recent bulletin of the Save the Redwoods League:

> Its water quality is one of the purest in the state, and because
> of this, the Smith and its tributaries are famed for their large runs
> of chinook and silver salmon, steelhead, and other native
> trout. . . . Twenty-seven rare and endangered plant species grow
> in the Smith River watershed. The large expanse of contiguous,
> unlogged areas provide habitat for 210 wildlife species including
> Roosevelt elk, black bear, mountain lion, black-tailed deer, eagle,
> fox and great blue herons.

It was a summer day a few years later when Marion and I
turned off Highway 101 at the tiny hamlet of Fort Dick and headed
eastward up the Smith River road. "The Van Deventer latchstring
is still out," Ruby had reassured us when we wrote that we'd be
driving up the Redwood Highway to Oregon.

Magnificent coast redwood, Douglas fir, and lowland fir
towered along our route, with windows in the vegetative screen

frequently revealing glimpses of the white waters or quiet pools of the Smith.

Soon the Van Deventer home came into view. Set far back from the road amid a sprawling orchard with a backdrop of forest, it perfectly matched Ruby's description. Her parents had purchased the place back in 1887.

The welcome was cordial. Ruby and Van were anxious that we stay long enough to feel the spell of the place and of the Smith River country. This was my first meeting with Van. We immediately became lifetime friends—all four of us. Van was also a descendant of early California pioneers. Much of his life had been spent in the big woods of northwestern California as an employee of the U. S. Department of Agriculture.

Then "The Project" was introduced. The outdoor tour could wait. Ruby's present life was centered on this tremendous undertaking. She was writing the *Flora of Del Norte County*. Pressed plants in herbaria sheets were stacked high in the living room. Botany manuals and journals were strewn around the work table area, together with paraphernalia including a dissecting scope, hand lens, calipers, and forceps.

"Here's the man who is responsible for all this," explained Ruby, holding aloft a worn blue book, *The Manual of California Flowering Plants* by Willis Linn Jepson. "Dr. Jepson loved this country. We'd put him up and I'd drive him all over the county. Finally he decided Del Norte needed a flora of its own and that I was the one to write it! Sometimes I wonder if I bit off too much, but I can't let him down now."

"Look at the start I've made." Ruby picked up a stack of finely written pages with many small drawings. "There are 500 species and races described here and many more to go. And now I want you to see what Van has done."

At another table Ruby began to gently lift sheets of watercolors out of a large box. Each one represented a Del Norte native plant, exquisitely portrayed. There must have been close to 200 of these paintings.

"And here's the artist," announced Ruby, putting her arm around Van, who was a little embarrassed by the raves over his work.

After standing in awe at all the work that went into the Project, viewing the garden was next. It was a typical north coast garden with lush lettuce and green vegetables screened from the hungry deer and rabbits, and rows of luscious berries ready for tasting. Then there was the apple orchard with gleaming fruit of several varieties. Some were still green and a couple of heavily-laden branches sagged to the ground. "Guess the old bear was here last night checking on the crop," observed Van unconcernedly.

Olive-sided flycatchers called "Oh, see me" from a tall redwood barn, tree swallows darted overhead, and distant drumming came from a pileated woodpecker. As for the barn swallows, I marked their nest right outside an upper bedroom window—just right for some filming.

A rich lore of Indians, pioneers, naturalist-explorers, and wildlife and botanical discoveries was recounted by Ruby and Van that first evening. In 1955 there were still a few old-timers and Yuroks, Tolowas, and Klamath left among the Van Deventers' friends and contacts. A few more days added to our visit might have allowed us to meet some of these vanishing people. What cruel losses a tight schedule can cost.

When we reluctantly said farewell to this intriguing couple a day later we felt a close bond of affection and mutual interest, and, of course we gave a promise to return soon.

After Dr. Jepson died in 1946, a new contact was needed by Ruby at the University of California Herbarium in Berkeley. She corresponded with a botanist named Robbins, but he too died after several years. Professor Rimo Bacagalupi then took on Ruby and the Del Norte flora. Dr. Rimo's Italian background made him a vivacious figure in a normally dull scientific environment. Soon he was examining many sheets of pressed plants (herbaria) sent from Del Norte for positive identification. Dr. Rimo, now retired, invited me to read the bulky file of correspondence between him and Ruby.

Dr. Bacagalupi made one trip to that section of Del Norte, enjoyed the Van Deventer's hospitality and tramped the woods with them. His visit brought the official blessing of a renowned institution to Ruby's project and helped her clarify more identification problems. As Ruby afterward wrote to him: "You'd have to live in a no-man's land [of science] to know how much it means to get such rich crumbs." Dr. Rimo chuckled as I read this one back to him later.

A long-planned visit to the bay area gave Dr. Rimo a chance to return their hospitality, as Dr. Jepson had done years before. A

Arthur and Ruby Van Deventer, 1968.

letter from Ruby following that visit read in part: "We haven't forgotten that very satisfactory evening in San Francisco at Veneto's restaurant or that ride over Twin Peaks."

Van and Ruby were by no means innocents abroad. The Spanish she taught at the local high school served her well on trips to Mexico. A genuine interest in people guaranteed the Van Deventers a warm reception south of the border too. What "rich crumbs" of Latin culture and anecdotes Ruby must have brought back for her students!

"Specimen Bacagalupi" was the form of address she used in a letter to Dr. Rimo in January 1961 announcing that she and Van were taking a vacation to Hawaii. Perhaps she remembered how she had been immobilized recovering from a broken ankle and compared it to this dear professional friend who was mostly confined to his cases of herbaria and shelves of books and papers.

"You mean we would get to stay right in bear and elk country? Maybe they'd even show me a mountain beaver!" This was the reaction of our twelve-year-old naturalist son Jim when I mentioned we might visit our Smith River friends in the summer of 1966.

After many days of vacationing throughout the Evergreen Empire of the Pacific northwest, we again turned up the Smith River highway. The Van Deventer home was a welcome sight. Jim could hardly wait for the car to come to a stop.

The Project had grown tremendously in those interim years, but our inspection would have to wait. Within minutes Van, Jim, and I were following a trail to a spring just within the nearby forest. Here lived one of the least known of western mammals, the mountain beaver or sewellel, a rodent that occurs along this north coast and in the high Sierra Nevada. Its burrows and runways penetrated the woodwardia fern, deer fern, salmon berry and huckleberry clumps.

"Yes, sewellels live here, but you seldom see them; they are nocturnal. Natives around here call them "boomers" for the call they give, but I'd say their booms are barely audible," explained Van.

This revelation about the sewellels left Jim somewhat disappointed. That evening he and I were out there in the evening damps with flashlights, but the boomers must have heard us coming and laid very low.

Arthur Van Deventer had served the U. S. Forest Service as a timber cruiser, then as ranger for many years before transferring to a Department of Agriculture white collar job. Listening to some of his adventures in the big woods soon wiped out Jim's disappointment over the sewellels. To climax his true stories, Van brought forth an ancient Colt revolver once carried by his grandfather, who came to California as a scout during the Mexican War. It bore a notch, but the victim of that shot is better left unnamed.

The big news Ruby had waited patiently to announce to us concerned the Project—it was nearly completed at last. Van had painted many more of the species treated.

"Now, I'd like you to read the whole thing and give me criticisms," said Ruby.

She must have read the answer in my expression of consternation. I had skimmed through just enough pages and seen enough of her scientific descriptions to realize it was far beyond my depth as a botanist. I would have had to take a refresher course with extensive lab work before I would feel qualified to fulfill such a task.

Instead we urged both Van and Ruby to make every effort to find a publisher or, failing that, to get a copy of the manuscript and store the paintings in a secure vault.

"I'll repeat what I said on your first visit, Paul," replied Ruby with a smile. "I promised Dr. Jepson only that I'd write the Flora of Del Norte, not that I'd publish it! Oh, I've got a few other things going around here," boasted our hostess. "Tomorrow we'll take you around and show you some of them and meet some interesting people."

Next morning it was off to Crescent City, the Del Norte county seat a few miles south on Highway 101. An old bent Indian woman was plodding along the roadside near Fort Dick. "She is a Yurok woman well up in her eighties and almost blind," said Ruby.

The subject of Indians, only second to wildlife in Jim's interests, led Ruby to elaborate on her Indian acquaintances. The old generation was dying out fast, and she regretted so few young people followed the traditions.

At the Del Norte County Historical Museum* in downtown Crescent City, Ruby the interpreter took over. It had been the enthusiasm of Van and Ruby that helped to launch this museum.

* At this writing the Del Norte County Historical Museum, located on H Street near the courthouse in Crescent City, is open May to September.

The curator at that time, Mrs. Ruth Roberts, patiently waited to co-lead our tour of the place.

The room devoted to the foods, artifacts, and culture of the northwest coast Indians—the Yuroks, Tolowas, and Klamath— would do justice to a bigger institution. Mrs. Roberts knew many of these people personally and made them come alive for us. She spoke of one Yurok woman, a centenarian, who still hobbled down from her cottage each day to visit the fishermen at the mouth of the Klamath and to carry home a donation.

Then someone mentioned the Old Lighthouse,* now an historic monument. Ruby and Van had managed to find a couple of Indian people to live there as custodians. Jim jumped at that prospect, but unfortunately the tide was in and we would have to return someday at low tide. Nevertheless, it was a day filled with Del Norte discoveries and history brought alive.

In the spring of 1968 I returned to Del Norte with a grim mission of fact-finding and picture-taking, one that would make me most unwelcome to many of the natives. A Redwood National Park† had been proposed for a large strip of coastal northern Humboldt and Del Norte counties. It was being bitterly opposed by lumber interests and by many of those who lived from logging, milling, and related income. It took a brave or foolish person to sport a Sierra Club emblem or similar motif in the woods.

Ruby and Art Van Deventer probably suspected my purpose when I wrote ahead. Nevertheless, they responded with the customary warm invitation and promised to pick me up at the Crescent City airport.

En route I stopped over at Arcata where a friend taught an environmental class at Humboldt State College (now California State University, Humboldt), a favorite school for foresters and wildlife management students.

---

* The Old Lighthouse at Battery Point, Crescent City, is open from May to September, but access to the light is subject to the tide.

† Redwood National Park was established by Congress on October 2, 1968. This longitudinal park extends from a wide block east of Orick up the coast and inland south of Jedediah Smith State Redwood Park, not far from the South Fork of the Smith River. It was originally authorized for 58,000 acres, but essential watershed purchases have brought it to some 75,000 acres. It borders several state redwood parks, which continue under state jurisdiction. The Smith River National Park proposed by the Save the Redwoods League and other supporters would also extend this national park through to the northwest coast at Crescent City.

Two days of observations in the field with my friend's class briefed me pretty thoroughly. For extremes, we viewed the infamous Arco Cut of redwoods near Patrick's Point State Park, the gruesome scene that helped convert Congress and a few million citizens. In fairness we also visited the "forests of the future" exhibits displayed by the lumber interests along Highway 101.

If the pro-park people won, many of these students might never work in private forestry. But these woods jobs were often seasonal and irregular. Perhaps they could get on the steady payroll of the U. S. Forest Service or the National Park Service.

Van's friendly greeting was most welcome at the airport. As a city dude with a camera bag slung over one shoulder, I imagined that I was getting some dark looks. Ruby had sent excuses for staying home; she was no longer the robust woman we had known.

A number of Del Norte folks, mindful of the contributions of this teacher-historian-botanist, had managed to have a redwood grove and little picnic spot on the Smith River named the Ruby Van Deventer County Park. Ruby was present at the dedication.

The chief purpose of my solo trip was soon revealed to these friends. How could I conceal it? They were sympathetic, to my intense relief. This represented much soul-searching on the part of Van the forester, who described the locations of current logging in that area and invited me to take their four-wheel drive vehicle to get pictures.

"We have a confession too," said Ruby, near the verge of tears. "We're selling a few more of the big redwoods up there in back, but there will be plenty of trees left for a screen. We hope our conservation friends will accept it."

The carnage I viewed the next day at the scene of recent logging was pretty terrible. Everything but the prime logs was left lying in gruesome piles. Waste, waste, waste. "There's no place they can afford to haul the other downed wood," explained Van later. "We desperately need a pulp mill in Crescent City."

During that last evening with the Van Deventers I discovered there had been no progress toward publication of the Flora. but there would soon be a new series of demands on Ruby's knowledge and expertise!

"Have you talked to Ruby Van Deventer?" was among the first responses from Del Norte officials and residents when the historians and natural resource teams of the new Redwood

National Park took to the field. Soon they were telephoning, writing, and beating paths to that fountainhead of knowledge—the home of Ruby and Van. Staff botanists could be seen carrying plant presses bulging with local collections for Ruby's help in identifications!

Stephen D. Veirs, Jr., research scientist for the National Park Service, wrote me warmly of his association with the Van Deventers and of their valuable services. I quote his closing sentence: "I will always remember the happy and congenial ranch house on the north bank of the Smith River where Ruby and Van welcomed the world and warmly changed the lives of passersby and botanists alike."

Generous offers for the old place which would have enabled them to live comfortably in town were stoutly refused. It was being saved for a grandson and his family to take over someday.

Our goodbyes following that visit (Ruby's fond embrace in her garden and a firm handshake from Van at the airport) left me depressed. I doubted that we'd share another such joyous event. Then I remembered how productive their lives had been—how many monuments of local interpretation and goodwill they would leave behind. Ruby passed away in 1974, Van in 1977. How fortunate we were to have known them.

NOTE: The *Flora of Del Norte County* manuscript remains unpublished. It reposes on the shelves of the Botany Department at California State University, Humboldt, at Arcata. Each decade following its completion brought drastic changes in the nomenclature and classification of California native plants which would have made revision and publication that much more difficult. However, many of the rarer plants collected by Ruby are in the Jepson Herbarium at the University of California at Berkeley. Van's flower paintings are in the custody of a family member. Dr. James Payne Smith, professor of botany at Humboldt, has compiled a master checklist from Ruby's notes and hopes that it will be published someday as an annotated checklist, along with a biographical sketch of Ruby and with one of Van's paintings.

The Naturalist's Naturalist:
Joshua Aaron Barkin

SOMETHING WAS backing up traffic on a main street of Pacific Grove that April afternoon in 1974. The cause seemed to be gawkers leaning out of car windows and calling back to drivers and other passengers. The distraction: a group of assorted adults and children examining something in the gutter. No, there didn't appear to be a body lying there.

The beat patrol came along and stopped to investigate. One policeman got out and walked over to the scene. There he saw a man wearing a Smokey Bear outfit and packing a knapsack. He was kneeling to point out something in the gutter. His followers were crowded around in various positions; some wore binoculars, others carried books, while a couple held hand lenses.

With a broad grin the officer waved on the curious motorists. "It's nothing, Joe," he reported back to his companion. "Just one of those ranger fellows with a class looking for something in the gutter. This is a switch from studying trees or bird watching—they probably belong to that bunch of rangers down at Asilomar.* I just wish they'd stay off the main streets!"

The officer couldn't be blamed for not recognizing interpretive specialist Josh Barkin, dean of the East Bay Regional Park District's naturalist force, originator of the "gutter walk" for urban nature students, the "hundred-inch hike," and innovator of other unique methods for introducing people to their environment.

Just how much nature can you expect to find in the average city gutter (one not recently hosed down)? The answer is amazing. All one needs to hold a group of curious people spellbound for an hour or so are the imagination and communication skills of a Josh Barkin.

First there were the cigarette butts: Josh described the great industry that produced them, the vast tobacco fields, the multimillion dollar costs and lethal effects on so many consumers, many of whom also were confirmed litterbugs! Some of these same people even sought special foods for better health, he added with a touch of irony.

Someone found a plastic six-pack beverage carrier. "Oh, oh," exclaimed Josh. "A lot of our precious oil goes to make those things, but the worst part is what happens with them afterward. Throw-away plastic holders are strangling ducks and seabirds and even fish. Better that this one wound up in the gutter!"

"Look, a flower growing in that crack in the curb!" called out a youngster. Josh hailed him for this discovery, and again gathered a circle of rapt listeners.

"How did the dandelion get its name?" he asked. "That's right—from the lion-tooth leaves. But did you know those leaves have fed millions of poor people since earliest times? Here's one that's gone to seed. Somebody blow on the head. Look, a company of parachutists is off to invade new soil. Wonder how far the wind could take them?"

A handful of discarded peanut shells was next on the treasure hunt. "Those remind me of George Washington Carver, the black

* The Asilomar Conference Center at Pacific Grove on the Monterey Peninsula is situated on state park land. It is regularly selected as a conference site by many organizations. On this occasion it was the first national conference of the Western Interpreters Association and the Association of Interpretive Naturalists.

scientist who found 300 uses for the peanut and discovered 150 products from the sweet potato. He also made cellophane from pine cellulose, and paper, paint, tiles, and shingles from milk— think what one gifted man can do!"

Ah, animal life at last. A minor trash dam had backed up enough water to attract honey bees. Josh grew even more eloquent as he extolled the virtues of the bee, but was rudely interrupted when a child found a stream of ants. The remains of a once lovely monarch butterfly were being laboriously carried back to the den somewhere across the sidewalk.

"Ants are scavengers that help clean our forests and farms as well as city gutters," explained the guide. "Did you know they live the longest of all insects? Let's follow them over into that vacant lot."

We did follow Josh Barkin to the end of his gutter walk, as we had followed him on other types of walks in the East Bay Regional Parks, enthralled, amazed, and perhaps a bit envious of his store of knowledge, philosophy, poetry, and magical power to captivate listeners. What background, what experiences and secrets of his earlier years had produced this sensitive, effective, naturalist teacher?

Joshua Aaron Barkin was born June 23, 1918, near the end of World War I, to a family of struggling European immigrants in Detroit, Michigan, where his father worked at the Ford Motor Company. When he was a child they moved to Staten Island, New York, after his father's severe illness. There they struggled to exist on the income of a small restaurant they opened, but his father found time for reading, music, and the arts, and instilled this love in his son. Josh always remembered his father's large library, a collection of literary works in several languages.

Young Josh developed another passion, nature, which was stimulated greatly after the family moved to Staten Island. There a neighbor, William T. Davis, an entomologist who had collected for the Staten Island Museum, befriended this budding young naturalist.

The youngster was so determined to have a "wilderness" experience that one day he took blankets and food and made his way to the Palisades Parkway along the Hudson River, where he camped overnight. Fortunately means were found to send him to a summer youth camp in the New York countryside. By that time he had joined the Woodcraft Rangers on Staten Island.

Tragedy hit the family when Josh was about ten years old. His father died suddenly, and his mother was forced to give up the restaurant and seek menial jobs. The 1930s depression hit hard and Josh was turned over to his mother's relatives, hard-working immigrants who found little time for culture. His father's library disappeared and he lost contact with the Staten Island naturalist who had befriended him. His paternal uncles deserted and ignored Josh, so he lost his remaining childhood role models. This deeply sensitive young boy with such great potential found himself in a lonely world indeed. A period of frustration followed these deep personal losses.

A brighter horizon dawned with a move to California at age fifteen. In Oakland he and his mother ran a small grocery store, where Josh worked throughout high school and college. Josh entered Oakland's Technical High School and was encouraged to develop his musical talents. Because a childhood accident had weakened his left wrist he had taken up the violoncello as a means of strengthening those muscles.

Cellist Barkin and a group of young musicians became part of an Oakland All-City Youth Orchestra and soon achieved great popularity in the east bay. While in high school he formed a string trio with friends and got his first job playing in a dining room in the elegant old Hotel Oakland. Upon entering the University of California at Berkeley, Barkin joined the University Symphony and became a well-known chamber music and string quartet cellist. Later his interest in Baroque music led to the formation of the first local Baroque concert ensemble in the east bay.

Liberal arts was the major Josh selected at Berkeley because of his love of culture, music, and literature—and perhaps because he had teaching in mind. But friends and relatives urged him to study science as the road to success, and so the young musician-naturalist did major in the sciences. But Josh wasn't made for laboratory courses. He was a naturalist of living things, a communicator, and an artist.

When World War II and the illness of his mother interrupted his studies he needed to work full time, so he went to work in the shipyards like thousands of others. After the war his mother's continued illness and his work in the grocery store made study impossible.

The call of the sea had somehow reached Josh Barkin. He was already an experienced sailor of small boats. Throughout his twenties he had sailed his own twenty-four-foot sloop on San Francisco Bay, having taught himself navigation and chart reading. He had thought of joining the Coast Guard even at that time, but couldn't leave the store. Now, with his life-long buddy, Edward Ormondroyd, he went to sea—Edward on oil tankers and Josh on the Red Stack tugs.

As a slight, not too robust man, he found the tug boat chores pretty hard at first. But he toughened up and even got used to the language of the other deckhands and stevedores. He found their coastal runs up to Coos Bay exciting—storms and all. What an experience for this gentle musician, nature man, scholar, and philosopher!

Whales, porpoises, seabirds, tugs, and tugboat people lost out when Josh came ashore and took a job. Perhaps he had missed the close access to the hills and the kindred souls he met on the trails, as well as his cello and musical group.

In the 1950s Josh was working in a lamp factory. He and Edward Ormondroyd began a serious study of natural history, tramping the Berkeley hills, bird watching and studying wildflowers and butterflies. In addition to music, they read insatiably the literature of classical natural history, from Elbert White, W. H. Hudson, and Charles Kingsley to John Burroughs, Emerson, and others.

They also became interested in scientific farming and studied the work of Louis Bromfield and his Malabar Farm for soil conservation and organic farming. In 1954 they thought of moving to a farm. This was the dream that later inspired Josh to urge the East Bay Regional Park District to develop a nineteenth-century farm, and may have helped to create Ardenwood Farm at Newark, which was opened in 1985.

In 1956 Josh decided to learn more methodically, and among other studies attended the Audubon Camp of California. Memories of the Woodcraft Rangers returned. He always remained an "amateur," he said—a "lover of natural history"—and his boyhood dream was about to become a reality. A natural-born teacher, artist, and performer, he was on his way back to the quiet world of nature.

"What a privilege to spend your day in the park and get paid for it!" Josh must have thought to himeslf more than once as he exchanged greetings with regional park employees on his walks. It didn't seem fair that he should have to return to the city and the lamp factory each Monday morning. So one day in 1960, when the factory was moving to Tennessee, he decided to stay in Berkeley and become a naturalist.

He packed his knapsack and started out for the regional park office up on the hill. Along his route he met a small child who asked what he had in the sack. "Something to read, something to eat, and something to wear," replied Josh. The child paused a minute and finally asked, "Are you going to seek your fortune?"

Josh long afterward said, "I immediately fell in love with that child." He may have realized that touching the lives of thousands of children would be part of his new fortune. Josh was immediately hired and assigned to a general maintenance job at Tilden Park. It was just another lucky stroke that teamed him up with the remarkable man in charge of Tilden programs.

Jack Parker, a trained forester and surveyor with a natural love of nature and children, had been leading walks and giving programs at Tilden since the late 1940s. Jack and his sympathetic wife Martha ("Boots") were established in converted Civilian Conservation Corps (CCC) residential quarters at the Tilden Park Nature Area. Jack had purchased a regulation ranger uniform and had attended ranger and interpretive training conferences when time permitted. Occasionally he assisted the naturalist teacher hired by the Oakland public schools, who operated from a classroom in another converted CCC building.

Jack was quick to recognize the potential in his new hire. Josh just bubbled with enthusiasm for his natural surroundings and wanted to communicate this spirit together with a few pertinent facts to any visitor who contacted him. One day Parker took him for a four-hour "nature hike" (actually the hiring interview for the assistant naturalist position). Jack became even more convinced that he'd discovered a rare human resource in Josh.

So maintenance man Josh soon found himself promoted to assistant park naturalist, and then park naturalist after completion of his probationary period in 1961. After years of experimentation Josh had found his element. Park visitors, his co-workers, and district administrators would all agree on that.

"Let's not try to supervise this man too closely. Give him a chance to try out some of his ideas and we're all going to benefit," was the gist of what Jack Parker told the big bosses. Among Josh's first innovations was the nature backpack, sometimes referred to by acquaintances as his "bag of tricks." This equipment was introduced for Josh's own use on nature walks. I cannot now enumerate all the contents, but conspicuous among them were: a small insect net, a trench shovel or trowel, hand lens, glass or plastic containers for small animals collected, a few field guides, soil auger, tape, mirrors, bird call, and more.

Each of these items came into use during a typical walk with naturalist Barkin. Things like the dip net for aquatic insects or the butterfly net might be loaned to a youngster to collect specimens under Josh's watchful supervision, but only to show the other participants and then release. A favorite Indian food could be sampled at the shallow man-made ponds en route to Jewel Lake, where Josh would use his sharp scout knife to carefully slice a young cattail stem and pass samples to willing tasters. The prolific cattails could stand some reduction.

After the walk or on rainy days, visitors would crowd into the tiny nature center, also converted from one of the old CCC buildings. Here Josh, Jack, and co-worker Marge Hutchinson exhibited some discreetly collected examples of plants, invertebrates, reptiles, and amphibians of the Tilden Nature Area. The *Tilden Nature News,* a Barkin brainchild, covered many events of the season and the nature programs. It soon achieved wide circulation among the park lovers and schools of the east bay.

Nature programs or interpretation were to make a great upward surge, probably beyond the dreams or expectations of Jack or Josh or their superiors. A brilliant park planner, William Penn Mott, Jr., became general manager of the East Bay Regional Parks in 1962. One of his goals was a district-wide system of visitor centers and programs staffed by trained interpreters.

One of Mott's initial steps was to engage Christian Nelson, a creative planner and organizer of visitor centers and interpretive programs. Nelson took charge of a new interpretive department of the park structure, and immediately a third naturalist, Dick Angel,* was hired at Tilden. Parker left the district in 1964, and

---

* Angel had been a school camp naturalist and high school biology teacher who became a district sales manager for *World Book Encyclopedia.* He often spent time at the Tilden Nature Area while waiting for late afternoon or evening appointments, and it was there that he met Josh. It was a meeting of kindred souls, and a friendship began that was to last as long as life itself. Eventually he recruited Josh to take a training class to become a *World Book* representative. However, the salesman became sold instead, and when an opening on Josh's staff for another naturalist was created, he joined the East Bay Regional Park District staff.

Josh waş promoted to resident naturalist at Tilden, moving with his wife Pearl into the modest living quarters.

As resident naturalist planning a bay cruise for youth classes, Josh was looking for a ship. Bill Mott told him to borrow the *Alma* from the State Parks. He then joined the Alma Sea Scouts and Friends of the *Alma* and spent many overnights sanding, scraping, and reconditioning the *Alma,* but he never got to borrow it. However, he did plan a Jack London trip for bay studies to Alviso and Petaluma Creek on the *Alma* for the Sea Scouts. The scouts took the Jack London trips after they acquired a motor, but Josh wasn't with them on those trips. Instead, he sailed on the *Alma* in the Master Mariner's Regatta of 1970. (The *Alma* is now berthed at the State Maritime Park in San Francisco.)

On one memorable shopping trip in Berkeley Josh and his wife Pearl stopped to admire some animal puppets. "Why not use something like this to teach nature?" asked Josh. Pearl thought they might. They went to the Berkeley Public Library immediately and checked out some books, including *How to Make a Puppet*

Josh Barkin and students (East Bay Regional Parks photo).

Theater. All the designs, characters, etc., came from the information in those books. Dick Angel built the puppet theater, and another Barkin teaching innovation—the Nature Puppet Theater—became a reality.

A theme for a puppet show was soon found: "Lester Litterbug Learns a Lesson." Josh and Pearl began to produce puppet characters such as Lester (the bad guy who turned good), Penny Pincushion, Naturalist Ned, Samuel Snake, Maud and Claud Caterpillar, Myrtle the Turtle, Inchy Inchworm, and others. They even bought their own materials, perhaps fearing such a request might completely upset a dour accountant. The staff auditioned for voice roles and a proper musical accompaniment was found. The whole show was then put on tape.

In ensuing years thousands of grownups and children sat spellbound by the rampages of Lester and swift detection and justice meted out by park rangers and the "good guys and gals." A small portable theater was fashioned to bring the show to outlying parks. Josh took his demonstration to conferences in other cities and even to distant states. Unfortunately nobody ever came up with an estimate of how many park litterbugs were turned from their evil ways after exposure to this show. Other puppet shows with environmental themes soon followed.

Naturalist Josh was to conceive yet another unique program, one that would allow his spiritual self full play and to encourage church people to "husband" God's earth as had the Indians. With the help of Dennis Kuby, a Berkeley clergyman, he initiated a "God in Nature" series at Tilden in spring and fall. Josh gave up a part of each Sunday, his day off, for this very special activity. Attendance was kept small. This little group under the trees never resembled a camp meeting nor drew protests from lurking atheists or others who nowadays attack any quasi-official religious public service.

Josh could see God in nature and the out-of-doors, as do so many people who never enter houses of worship nor read holy books. His walks and talks were sprinkled with relevant quotations from the Bible, the Koran, the American Indian view of nature, and great minds of literature and philosophy down through history.

Blind and other handicapped visitors to the regional parks presented a challenge to this humanitarian naturalist. Wheelchair-bound visitors deserved a more intimate contact with the Tilden

Nature Area than just being wheeled to the Little Farm, the visitor center, and down the road to Jewel Lake. Together with his superiors and park construction people, Josh laid out a boardwalk nature trail through the "swamp" en route to Jewel Lake. Here the handicapped visitor and others could overlook the little stream with its mating or egg-laying salamanders, occasional fish, and footprints of night-prowling raccoons. In spring a chorus of thrush, vireo, warbler, grosbeak, and other bird songs in the alders and willows overhead greatly enhanced this little adventure.

Those who couldn't hear bird voices or even the voices of the naturalists because of hearing impairment also needed a fair break, Josh insisted. This led to the addition of David Lewton to the district interpretive force. Dave was an expert in signing and was soon entertaining hearing-impaired visitors throughout the park system, and teaching signing to other interpreters.

General Manager Mott,* his planners, Chris Nelson, and some of the interpreters realized that a modern visitor center and naturalist staff headquarters was desperately needed. A site in the Tilden Nature Area was favored, but immediately a number of environmentalists and groups demanded another site because of the added traffic it would bring there. If built at Tilden, a grove of older eucalyptus would have to be cleared. These trees held poignant memories for Josh and others, so he joined the protestors—at least in spirit and prayers. Perhaps they could have divided the visitor center among two or three sites from Tilden to Redwood Park. But eventually the public resistance was overcome and construction began at the Nature Area site. It was a grievous spiritual and moral blow for Josh, though he was compelled outwardly to accept it.

"Help! Help! We're swamped! Weekdays are booked solid, with classes from 9 a.m. to 3 p.m., and after that, with Scouts, Campfire Girls, Brownies, Bluebirds, and Cubs. We can scarcely find time for lunch and pit stops. If anyone gets sick, Marge Hutchinson has to leave the office and the phone to do tours." This was the gist of an urgent memo to supervising naturalist Chris Nelson in April 1966. It wasn't news to Chris, who had often been drafted to take a tour or a program somewhere. Nelson and

* Mott left the district in 1967 to head the California Division of Beaches and Parks under Governor Reagan. Richard Trudeau served as general manager from 1969 to 1985.

Mott were constantly at work on the board to authorize more naturalist positions. Such public response spelled a clear need!

Meanwhile Josh suggested to Chris another simple but exciting activity for children on naturalist tours: give them some plaster and molds to record the tracks of deer, raccoons, and other animals along the trail to take home as souvenirs of their experience. Great idea! Approved.

But added to the swelling workload at the Nature Area came the barrage of urgent invitations—demands on Josh's time in almost every day's mail: Mr. Barkin, can you help us set up a new course in marine oceanography for our elementary classes? Mr. Barkin, we want you to address our hospital staff on therapeutic programs from your field. Mr. Barkin, you are invited to help train our Sacramento State College class in camp counseling. Mr. Barkin, we need you at our YMCA summer camp staff training again this year. Mr. Barkin, the Red Cross needs you to train staff and volunteers in convalescent home therapy.

The old adage, "If you want a job done, give it to a busy person," was exemplified by Josh Barkin. He was persuaded in 1969 to accept the presidency of the Golden Gate Audubon Society. As Josh plunged into this voluntary job, it became no small burden added to his crowded life. Membership soon soared upward through President Barkin's "soft sell" recruiting of many of his followers. He continued this labor of love for two productive years, during which time he also raised the enthusiasm and educational objectives of the chapter.

Then there were the enthusiastic letters that followed Barkin's contributions to the American Camping Association at Asilomar, together with demands for his appearance at their next conference in southern California. These were typical of the growing crescendo of invitations for this gifted naturalist, educator, and philosopher following each public appearance.

California's first people were another subject close to the hearts of both Josh and Pearl Barkin. Include California Indian cultures in district interpretive programs, naturalist Barkin urged. Rebuffs from certain district decision-makers who didn't think it worthwhile only added fuel to his determination. Josh finally won his argument: Indian handcraft lessons appeared on some Tilden programs, and Indian foods were sometimes gathered and prepared.

When Coyote Hills Regional Park with its ancient Indian

mounds went into operation, both Josh and Pearl were ecstatic. Barkin could not be physically present at these Ohlone campsites to greet visitors, but he was proud to help the district locate and hire an Indian as one of the local ranger-naturalist staff.

A text for the greeting sign at the Indian mounds was later written by Josh and Pearl:

WELCOME!

Once the forefathers of the Ohlone Indians lived here.
Here is where they are buried.
They lived in harmony with nature, and all
Living things were their brothers.
The Earth and all its creatures were sacred.
The Indian world was a religious world—
A world of the spirit.
Let your spirit and theirs intermingle.
Walk gently.
Walk with reverence.
It will give you peace.

The magic name of Josh Barkin was most associated with the Tilden Nature Area, although by the mid-1960s a staff of several dedicated men and women naturalists were conducting programs. The title of supervising naturalist had been given Barkin for a while, but supervision and the accompanying paper work proved to be bitter daily pills for Josh. Naturalist Ron Russo had graciously agreed to handle the paper work for him, and Josh was later given a unique title of "Interpretive Specialist," which permitted him to choose his own subjects, times, and locations of walks and talks, and placed great emphasis on training his staff of naturalists.

Some of the younger scientifically-trained district interpreters may have found it difficult to completely accept Josh's philosophies and folksy approach. Scientific names and classifications would only obfuscate his interpretations, he often said. His great interest lay in interpretation for children and teaching interpretive methods to young naturalists and teachers. Everything is connected to everything else. He went for understanding relationships and processes rather than labels. One of his favorite phrases was, "You start with entertainment and end with learning." He emphasized the Socratic method of question and answer as a teaching technique along with humor.

Josh's interpretations, with their reverence for nature in all its forms, brought a new outlook to younger students and to park naturalist trainees beyond the bay area. It was instant acceptance and success whenever he appeared at teachers' seminars and at training sessions for the California Department of Parks and Recreation, the National Park Service, and the U. S. Forest Service. Invitations for naturalist Barkin to speak and participate in seminars and training sessions across the United States and Canada eventually threatened to monopolize his working and personal time. Each agency, park district, and university gladly defrayed all his travel and living expenses and reimbursed the park district for his lost services. Testimonials to Josh's accomplishments in this field are reflected in a bulky file of letters Pearl Barkin kindly permitted me to read. I will quote only from two of these:

"On behalf of both our training group and staff, may we extend our thanks for Mr. Barkin's time and effort and, more importantly, the impact his presentation made on our training program and its participants. His creative, innovative approach to the interpretive field will, we're sure, carry over in many of our new rangers throughout their careers in park service," wrote William Penn Mott, Jr., Chief, California Department of Parks and Recreation, to Richard Trudeau.

"Josh has touched the lives and careers of many NPS interpreters—some profoundly, like me—and through them many thousands of park visitors. . . . To me, Josh Barkin is one of the greatest interpreters alive today," testified a letter to Trudeau from Ronald G. Thoman, training specialist for the National Park Service, after Barkin worked with a ranger class at the Albright Training Academy at Grand Canyon, and at the Stephen T. Mather Training Center in Harpers Ferry, West Virginia, in 1977.

Finally the demands from the National Park Service became so insistent and the educational program outlines so rewarding that Josh asked the park district for a year's "sabbatical leave." He planned to use a trailer to tour the United States, giving training presentations at many national parks, monuments, and historic sites. Unknown to many, Josh had become a close friend of the "father of interpretation," Freeman Tilden, who was grooming him to take Freeman's place as consultant of interpretation to the National Park Service.

But fate decreed otherwise. For some time his sheer passion and dedication to his goals blinded and deceived Josh, pushing

Josh Barkin makes a point (East Bay Regional Parks photo).

him on despite a growing internal affliction. This illness overpowered him after he had given a session at the famous Arizona-Sonora Desert Museum near Tucson. He had to be rushed back to the bay area for treatment.

Josh Barkin was forced to give up his brilliant career within a year and go into retirement. He passed away in April 1982. Regional park visitors in the east bay were deprived of the "Barkin experience" at Tilden, and teachers, rangers, and interpreters across North America would no longer be thrilled and influenced by this naturalists' naturalist.

Josh had a storehouse of famous quotes that always surfaced on the right occasion. One from a favorite of his, Henry David Thoreau, was read at his memorial service by Chris Nelson in hopes it would have reflected perfectly Josh's feelings toward death: "Every blade in the field, every leaf in the forest lays down its life, in season, as beautifully as it was taken up."

The following verses from William Wordsworth I have selected from a scrapbook of Josh's favorite poetry and quotations, which he sprinkled liberally through his interpretive talks:

One impulse from a vernal wood
May teach you more of man;
Of moral, evil, and of good,
Than all the sages can.

Sweet is the lore which nature brings;
Our meddling intellect
Misshapes the beauteous forms of things;
We murder to dissect.

Enough of science and of art;
Close up those barren leaves;
Come forth, and bring with you a heart
That watches and receives.

Bird Bander of Benicia: Emerson Austin Stoner

AN AVOCATION WITH birds which developed into a distinguished career in ornithology received early encouragement when young Emerson Stoner's father built a bluebird house in the 1890s. It was placed in a big oak in their Des Moines, Iowa, yard. The bluebirds responded, as did the boy. There were trips to the local library as well as his own purchases of identification books. One of the latter was an 1899 edition of O. T. Miller's *The First Book of Birds* with the preface, "This book is intended to interest young people in the ways and habits of birds, and to stimulate them to further study."

The quantity and quality of bird guides available then doesn't begin to compare with what we have in the 1980s. The few pictures were photographs of museum mounts taken in black and white. Colored pictures were making an appearance, however, and the Iowa boy collected a large number of the colorful A. W. Mumford prints of 1900, not only of birds but a broad spectrum of natural subjects.

133

When his parents separated, Emerson and his mother took up residence in Des Moines' Greenwood Park Station, where she became postmistress and he helped operate the concession. The world of nature with its seasonal changes was literally at his back door in this park location during the years 1904–1919. This was the site where he began egg study and collection as well as taxidermy. A lifetime of field note diaries commenced in 1906 with the entry, "Received my oological tools by mail this morning." After taking a taxidermy course of forty lessons by mail, he was awarded a diploma from the Northwestern School of Taxidermy, Omaha, Nebraska, in 1912. An entry in 1913 reads, "I mounted a Great Horned Owl with wings spread, and this specimen brought me many congratulatory remarks from customers; so much so that I felt I had indeed become a first-class taxidermist."

He mounted a great many birds from the local casualties that came his way: robin, blue jay, bluebird, brown thrasher, catbird, rose-breasted grosbeak, Baltimore oriole, green heron, screech owl, etc. Young naturalist Emerson thus had an early acquaintance with bird anatomy and the distribution of feather tracts. He also learned to pierce and drill an egg shell and neatly blow out the contents with a water pipe, then to write the date clearly on the shell!

Moving to California in 1914 had its drawbacks—there were too many specimens to pack, so he had to part with all those that did not fit in and around his mother's treadle sewing machine in the train's baggage car!

Once might say that Iowa's loss was California's gain. Emerson Austin Stoner came west to attend the University of California at Berkeley in September 1914. Lacking a chemistry course, he went to night school to complete the requirement. Then, feeling "too old [at twenty-two] to commence as a university freshman," he took a business course at Heald's Business College in Oakland. It was there he met the future Mrs. Stoner in the person of Myrtle Eleanor Henderson. They were married in 1918. His shorthand, typing, and accounting skills secured a government position at the Benicia Arsenal that lasted from 1917 to 1957. These same skills, together with his equitable disposition and diligence, were used to serve many civic organizations over a lifetime.

Without a car in those early years at Benicia, the young couple walked and enjoyed the local wildlife. Emerson's territory grew to include Contra Costa County in addition to Solano County and beyond. The Stoners became active church members, Emerson joined service clubs and was elected to the school board, and as he delivered talks and published articles, more and more of the populace realized they had a naturalist among them. Here was the place to bring a sick or injured bird for consultation or care, or for a hunter to get an accurate identification or have his trophy mounted, or to bring a highway casualty to benefit scientific interests.

His California Fish and Game scientific collector's permit allowed him to collect a small, controlled number of non-game birds, nests, eggs, and mammals. A private museum slowly grew and expanded into a second floor. Scouts came to study for badges, and a cabinet of specimens, including butterflies and other insects, was donated to the school system. His own three children were proud to "show and tell" at school, passing along their father's knowledge.

Hearing that the U. S. Biological Survey had started a bird banding program to learn more about birds, their longevity and migration patterns, he applied and received one of the first permits, and commenced banding with government sparrow traps in 1920. He repeatedly called this time-consuming, non-paying, government-sponsored venture "a privilege," a chance to get well-acquainted with the feathered folk.

"Mr. Stoner is catching birds in his yard and putting rings on their legs!" one might imagine a school-age child saying. "I watched him take one out of a trap and squeeze on a band he said had the bird's number and official address. Then he wrote it all down in a book, and he says he'll send the notes to Washington, D.C."

Myrtle soon learned how to retrieve a trapped bird for her husband. Eventually their daughter Marjorie, who shared her father's appreciation for nature, was also federally- and state-licensed to band migratory birds.

Wild bird banding had become of major scientific use by the mid-1920s, and a new pursuit for scores of bird students from coast to coast. Not only were amazing long-distance records being made for strong flyers such as ducks, geese, terns, raptors, and shore birds, but also for the smaller, weaker songbird migrants of the Americas. As for the fast-mounting task of record keeping, the Biological Survey found itself facing a gargantuan task.

"We need to talk with one another, get together once in a

Emerson Stoner blows an egg (Marjorie Elmore photo).

while and compare notes," urged bander Emerson Stoner. He assisted in organizing the Western Bird Banding Association in January 1925, becoming a charter member, and was its president for the years 1954 and 1955. Willing workers were found to publish a journal of members' activities and findings. It was more than two decades later that I joined the group as a duck bander at Lake Merritt and made the acquaintance of Emerson Stoner.

Those shiny aluminum bird bands, particularly the larger sizes, occasionally wind up in strange places. They have been found adorning the anatomy of tribal beauties in remote locations. But a story that Emerson sent in to the organization's journal, *News from the Bird Banders*, in July 1949, caps them all. The following incident occurred when bands bore the terse inscription "Wash. Biol. Survey."*

"Dear Sirs," complained an irate farmer to the survey. "I shot one of your pet crows the other day and followed instructions attached to it. I washed it and boiled and served it. It was terrible. You should stop trying to fool the public with things like this."

Mist nets, mostly made by the Japanese, were a sensational breakthrough for bird banders in the 1950s after the Fish and Wildlife Service had approved their use. These almost invisible barriers to flight could be raised on slender poles to fifteen feet or more, then quickly lowered to release their struggling catches for banding.

Liberation from forty years of weekly work schedule came in 1957 when chief fiscal officer Emerson Stoner retired from civilian service at the Benicia Arsenal. Now he could really find enough time for the netting and banding, his research and writing, trips, and so on. By the fall of 1964 he had banded some 11,000 birds, including about 4,000 cedar waxwings, predominantly within the confines of his Benicia back yard. Of the waxwings he made a special study. A group of pepper trees bordering the residence yielded fruit that did not please the waxwings, so not only did the Stoners plant berry-producing shrubs such as toyon, pyracantha, and elderberry, but prevailed upon their friends for berry branch trimmings as supplements, draping them invitingly in season.

Myrtle was a little less understanding when it came to permitting the linnets to eat from their fruit trees. Birder Emerson was

* This story preceded the name change from Biological Survey to Fish and Wildlife Service during President Franklin Roosevelt's terms.

fascinated with the manner in which these linnets, or house finches, punctured and then "appeared to drink the juices of peaches, discarding any solids with a shake of the head." A few of these fruit-pickers wound up in the laboratory, where he analyzed their total menus. But it was the stomach contents of cedar waxwing casualties brought in that were a special project of Emerson's. Their sudden switch to selecting flower petals in spring when red berries were exhausted was most interesting. This information appeared in scholarly papers written by him.

A package addressed to Emerson Stoner from the Fish and Wildlife Service labeled "Contents: stomachs" threw the Benicia post office into an uneasy state one day. If it hadn't been their leading citizen-naturalist who turned up to claim it, they might have called out the postal inspector or police. Stoner had to explain that the package contained the stomachs of 200 shrikes (butcher-birds) that he'd offered to analyze for the government.

The axiom that a busy person always has time for more was again illustrated by Emerson when he volunteered to work for the Point Reyes Bird Observatory (PRBO).* Their headquarters in 1965 consisted of some old wooden buildings on the Palomarin Mesa across Marin County and west of Bolinas Bay and the village of that name. Certainly the appeal of the bird observatory was irresistible for a man like Emerson. They had begun from scratch when a helpful Point Reyes National Seashore superintendent had found them a home—a shack on an old sheep ranch on the road to the lighthouse. Then a young Fish and Wildlife ornithologist resigned from the Bird Banding Laboratory to take over this new, challenging project that paid only a token salary. A succession of young ornithologists and biologists followed his steps there.

It was a progressive move when the park administration shortly thereafter agreed to install the bird banders in the old school buildings of the Church of the Golden Rule at Palomarin. The park service even granted them small contracts to perform certain avifaunal research projects. Organizers and directors of the PRBO included such eminent ornithologists as Dr. L. Richard Mewaldt (California State University at San Jose), Dr. C. John

* Headquarters of the Point Reyes Bird Observatory is now at 4990 Shoreline Highway, Stinson Beach, CA 94970 (just west of the Audubon Canyon Ranch). Persons inquiring here will be directed to the Palomarin Field Station when station schedules permit.

Ralph (Johns Hopkins University), and Dr. Howard C. Cogswell (California State University at Hayward). Volunteers from all directions appeared to share in this exciting program, many of them trained students and graduates. Some set up novel operations, such as netting shore birds on migration along the beaches during hours of darkness.

Birdman Stoner occasionally assisted in manning the nets and banding the captures, sometimes in the chill winds and fogs of the site, but he was drafted for a greater responsibility. He became the first PRBO treasurer, serving until 1973, when Myrtle insisted that he retire.

How Emerson must have thrilled over some of those migrant bird captures brought into the little Palomarin laboratory for banding, weighing, and recording! Catches in fall frequently included tiny warblers and vireos, flycatchers, tanagers, and other species of the Central and Mississippi Flyways. Due either to miscalculations or powerful upper strata winds, these little migrants from the north found themselves on the Pacific Flyway and made landings on the Point Reyes Peninsula. New North American transit or "stray occurrence" records for the Pacific coast began to pile up at PRBO. In 1966 alone they banded 7,000 birds of 103 species at this station!

Another great banding venture, beginning in 1968, began to unfold before Emerson's scrutiny. Why not put a banding and observation crew on the Farallon Islands? This is a group of small islands some twenty-five miles west of San Francisco. The South Farallon has a powerful light and for years had housed a Coast Guard crew and their families. A site of lucrative sea bird egg collecting in earlier days, the islands had recently been declared a National Wildlife Refuge.

Unable to afford a warden on the Farallons, the Fish and Wildlife Service was sympathetic to the PRBO proposal. A cooperative Coast Guard transported a PRBO team, as well as provisions and equipment, promising to make periodic resupply trips every few weeks. This service was eventually taken over by the Oceanic Society as a public service.

This offshore oasis, with a weather-beaten cypress tree and a few shrubs, began to yield amazing results. Exhausted small bird migrants dropped in by the score, including an impressive list of eastern species, just like the peninsular station. Then there were the thousands of nesting sea bird species in spring and early summer to study, census, and record: cormorants, murres, puffins, auklets, and of course the dominant western gulls.

There were also serious disturbances, such as shooting from offshore boats toward the colony of stellar sea lions that loafed and bred on one beach. The PRBO team reported descriptions of those boats by radio to the Coast Guard and the Fish and Wildlife Service. Only a few were ever caught.

The Farallons experiment became a permanent, highly lucrative scientific operation. This team could observe from week to week the effects of massive disasters on sea birds and seals. Somehow all seemed to survive both the widespread impact of El Niño (which warmed the offshore currents), and one catastrophic oil tanker spill. By the date of this writing an elephant seal colony on the South Farallon has grown to more than 1,000 animals.

When treasurer Stoner reluctantly terminated his services to the Point Reyes Bird Observatory in 1973 its annual budget was nearly $100,000, membership was over 2,000, and active volunteers were counted by the score. Its scope of annual operations became divided into estuarine and coastal research, marine research, and landbird research, and would eventually extend into the American Arctic and the tropics.

As each December approached, it was time to organize another Christmas Bird Count, a project begun in 1930 by birdman Stoner in the fifteen-mile diameter greater Benicia area. Many Audubon groups had been doing it since 1900 in the east; Emerson himself had participated in Iowa in 1910. This operation grew in size, results, and fame until in 1979 fifty-one participants counted 34,733 individual birds of 133 species in this community along the Carquinez Straits and Suisun Bay. By 1985 the number of species was up to 157, placing this count within the upper three percent in all the United States.

The Birdman of Benicia would bring nationwide attention to this small portion of California through his prolific writings as well as by banding migrants and conducting bird censuses. A total of 229 contributions to both scientific and popular ornithological and nature journals and magazines was enumerated by his daughter Marjorie the year of his death (Marjorie is a University of California graduate and the wife of Professor Dana Elmore). Among these were two to *Audubon Magazine*, sixteen to its longtime predecessor, *Bird Lore*; *Nature* magazine, *Junior Natural History*, and sixty to *The Condor*, official journal of the Cooper Ornithologi-

Emerson Stoner, Ross' Goose, and child (Marjorie Elmore photo).

cal Society. In addition to these articles, for two years he also wrote a weekly column about the birds, mammals, and wildflowers of Solano County as guest columnist for the Benicia *Herald and New Era* newspaper. That explains why the lights often burned late in Emerson's study long after the birds, curious visitors, and family had retired.

Emerson Stoner characteristically gave much thought to the proper disposition of his natural history collection as he reached his eighties, and realized it must eventually find other homes. As mentioned, the Benicia public schools, always close to his heart, received common bird study skins and other nature materials that would enthrall and instruct both teachers and students for many years to come. The Point Reyes Bird Observatory selected a few valued specimens and periodicals. A truckload of bird skins and carefully packed eggs on two occasions were delivered to the Western Foundation of Vertebrate Zoology in Los Angeles. Some specimens dated back to his first collecting days in 1912. His prolific egg collection has become a valuable standard for comparing normal eggshells with those of a later, toxic era.

The devoted couple, fortunate indeed, celebrated Emerson's ninetieth birthday in 1982 together with their three children, ten grandchildren and seven great-grandchildren, and a few Benicia friends. Emerson's long, productive life came to an end on March 7, 1983. His dear Myrtle, life partner and helpmate, had passed away the preceding month.

Something Special:
Elizabeth Cooper Terwilliger

THE "PIED PIPER of California," Elizabeth Cooper Terwilliger, presents still another noteworthy example of a person trained for other careers who became so overwhelmed by the natural world that a life devoted to showing off its charm and to preaching its preservation became the only answer.

Could it have been some genes passed down from ancestors Daniel Boone, James Fennimore Cooper, and Kit Carson that surfaced to create this naturalist whose teachings and messages have reached hundreds of thousands of her fellow Americans? As she grew up on a Hawaiian sugar plantation and studied home economics and institutional management, did family or friends ever guess she would become a noted exponent of saving wild America?

It was the spell of the Golden State, while earning her R.N. from the Stanford University School of Nursing, and hiking in the

Sierra Nevada that determined what would dominate Elizabeth's interests and goals next to her own family. It was the need of her own children, in fact, that started "Mrs. T," as her students call her, on her career of nature education.

Mrs. T's method of introducing the natural environment to children and adults is described as multi-sensory. That really means imitating and interacting with her on a field trip as she demonstrates how to look, listen, touch, smell, and taste. This isn't unique; originally inspired by the American Indian, many generations of nature guides have done likewise. But Mrs. T's style is unique to her.

This was to be my first full flight in "tripping with Terwilliger" through a magnificent redwood forest and over the bonnie braes of western Marin County on a day in early April 1987.

In the get-together circle her followers flapped like large birds and called out to any feathered friends who might be up there. From her van she introduced us to stuffed creatures, all natural casualties, to demonstrate her famous bird-in-the-hand teaching methods. The circle of twenty-five adults represented many of the fifty states. Not only were there beginners but also those who had tripped with Terwilliger from bay shores through redwoods and over coastal hills to the ocean.

"Hi Buttercup!" called out Mrs. T as we set out across the first dewy meadow sprinkled with this flower. And a moment later, "Hi Strawberry! Come back for strawberries in June!"

The first giant redwood revealed a serpentine vine stem encircling the lower trunk—a stem a full hand in diameter. The foliage or any flowers borne by this vine are so high that it takes binoculars to distinguish them. It is none other than poison oak—chief nemesis of so many humans who would otherwise embrace nature and the wild.

"Something special!" Mrs. T plucked a bracken fern tip or fiddle, rolled it in her palm and tasted it. Several of her students did likewise. Bracken or brake is a circumpolar fern whose roots were also cooked and eaten by primitive people, but I'd advise caution in using these. Another edible grew close by for the leader to identify and demonstrate: miner's lettuce or Indian lettuce. Blessed are those of vegetarian preference; while they smacked their lips with pleasure, I would have added a little salad oil, or perhaps the crushed ant juice some Indians used to render such foliage tasty!

Ah, an old fallen log. What surprises may lie beneath such a hiding place? Mrs. T supervised while several willing students gently rolled it over. Suddenly she pounced and held up a tiny writhing animal.

"Look, a newt or salamander," proclaimed Mrs. T. "Look at the bright orange belly. Notice the eye color and pattern; compare it with your eyes. What happened to the front feet?" (Salamanders' front toes number only four.)

"Follow me. All inside and sit down, please," cried Mrs. T as we came to a tree circle surrounding the burnt-out remains of one of the giants felled in the late 1800s. When all were comfortably seated inside, silence was ordered so we could listen to the breezes rustling the new trees high above and listen for Woody Woodpecker. Woody didn't speak, but some of us thought of the era when Indians, elk, and giant grizzlies roamed through here, and nature was in balance.

Something triggered off one of Mrs. T's many anecdotes before we left this intimate circle within the circle. Once at a Christmas party given by some prominent Marin businesswomen who had invited Elizabeth as guest speaker, Elizabeth launched into a passionate plea to save more of Marin's open space at the sacrifice of more subdivisions and shopping centers. Some shocked reactions from the audience, even a whispered caution from the program chairman, only served to intensify the speaker's dramatic plea. Elizabeth still glows as she recounts the story.

Call notes of two tiny insect hunters, the creeper and western flycatcher, were heard as we resumed the walk. Mrs. T and several students imitated the flycatcher in his streamside haunts, but necks craned and lips tried in vain to locate the bark-clinging creeper somewhere overhead. The raucous calls of the stellar jay, who sees all, talks back, and is easily seen, came as a relief.

"Hi, Milkmaids! Hi, Adders-tongue! Hi, Slim Solomon!" cried Mrs. T as we met in turn these woodland-floor flowers. She was seeking the fairy-bells—"They light up the glade when the fairies come to dance"—but instead came upon a bright orange shelf fungus at the base of a tree. "Ah, here are the seats the fairies use when they watch their friends dance!"

The moss-covered remains of an old lumberman's camp were a signal for all to take log seats. A large square pit enclosed by low stone walls was a center of interest. "All right, you men, get a fire going here," commanded Mrs. T. "You ladies find a couple of stirring ladles and let's get this stew on!"

Thus we contemplated a crew of famished loggers swarming around their noon meal and, incidentally, wondered when Elizabeth would get to a lunch stop.

Mother Nature's forces had recently felled one of the second-growth giants just beyond this old camp. So huge was the root ball and the excavation it left that a small pool had formed which had to be investigated.

That much needed lunch stop did come about 12:30 p.m., when we crossed the county road, skirted the margin of an abandoned golf course, and settled down on the bank of a frog pond. Mister Frog didn't appear to greet us, despite Mrs. T's clear invitations, but did surface for a peek as we departed.

I managed to interview our leader during lunch while the others were busy eating and chatting. Her popular school field trips, extending from bayshore marsh through the redwoods to an ocean beach, deserved far more treatment than I would be able to cover.

As we got to the subject of tidepooling at Muir Beach, I quizzed Mrs. T on how she handled what looked like a delicate situation. Muir Beach is part of the Golden Gate National Recreation Area, and nudism is allowed on the small northern section where all the rocks and pools are found. "Oh, nudes are no problem. I just treat them casually. After all, they're part of nature too," she explained.

My good friend, fellow naturalist and artist Rex Burress, had tripped with Terwilliger across Marin to the beach and shared these impressions.

Muir Beach offered no embarrassment to Mrs. T and her elementary school children. As they filed across the beach they called out, "Hi, Mr. Seagull!" or "Hi, Mr. Crab," as they spotted the first crab peeking from beneath a rock. Mrs. T usually expanded these greetings into an appropriate ditty addressed to the subject. So when the class crossed the boundary ledge into the nude sunbathing territory, someone called out "Hi, Mr. Nudie!" or "Hi, Mrs. Nudie!" whichever was applicable. The unclothed generally waved and called back. End of that discovery.

Mrs. T pulled a purple shore crab out from under a rock and demonstrated how to hold it without getting nipped by a probing claw. Now was the time for a very different sort of sex lesson. "Examine the belly plate to see if it's a mother with an egg mass inside," ordered the leader. "If this isn't the case, it's a less interesting male specimen."

Tiny limpets clustered at the splash zone on the big rocks were easily examined. "If they have holes in the top they're keyhole limpets and suggest tiny volcanos. How do they feed, glued to the rock with no visible appendages?"

"Look, Mrs. T, a neat snail! It doesn't look icky like the ones in our garden. But it has closed its door."

"Look at that door. It looks like a sheet of brown plastic. We're lucky to find a moon snail. Snails are univalves or one-shelled and have doors for protection, just as we do at home," says Mrs. T. "Now let's look for some bivalves. Remember, they'd have two shells that fit tight together. Ah, there's a razor clam! Try prying it apart with your fingers. Of course you can't. It has a grip much stronger than your fist when you're trying to hide something from another prying person."

"Something special! Let's go up on the warm sand and build some river systems. Some of you are shivering a bit," Elizabeth said. She was among the first to plop down and begin excavating rivers and lakes. A small pail and toy shovels appeared, and all students joined the fun, some relaying water from higher waves.

"Look, now we're going to add man's water plan to all these natural waterways. We'll build a huge holding reservoir up here. Let's float little shell boats down the river; keep that water coming, you boy and girl rain clouds!

"Oh, oh! Jimmy and Mike, we need some villains to spoil this pretty picture. Quick, somebody build more cities near the mouth of the river and cross-hatch the sand for more farmland. We're going to need a lot more water. Big capital wants to send it all the way to Los Angeles. Mike and Jimmy start building dams along the river. Never mind the boaters and rafters and the migrant fish and wildlife! What do you think about that?

"Now we're going to build a volcano. California had plenty of them millions of years ago. One even erupted in your grandparents' time. Which one? Mount Lassen, that's right."

The miniature volcano rose swiftly as many little hands heaped on the wet sand. It needed a small core tunneled out and a vent in the summit. Mrs. T very quietly ignited some slow-burning, smoking paper which she deftly inserted in the tunnel.

Smoke rose from the little beach volcano. Students and teachers formed a ring around it and applauded. Even some of the sunbathers curiously watching from nearby called out congratulations. "Now let's flatten it in a massive earth movement, pick up that paper, and head for the bus," commanded Elizabeth. Another day's studies from bay marsh to redwoods and to seashore had sharpened thirty young minds. She makes learning fun!

This famous "Pied Piper of Marin," as some San Francisco *Examiner* writer once dubbed her, hasn't worked singled-handed in her crusade to introduce Marinites to nature around them. After tripping with Terwilliger that day I retraced the trail to her lair and met some of her pack of lovely, efficient, and enthusiastic female docents—and one or two friendly young men.

The Terwilliger Nature Education Center is housed in one of a number of primary school buildings, pods in the round, just off the Paradise Cove Road in Corte Madera. The exhibits are eye-grabbers done in modern style but with only one live animal on the occasion of our visit—a large well-fed king snake. Two additional magnetic nature vans visit schools in eleven bay area counties, conveying Mrs. T's philosophy to 60,000 youngsters with hands-on programs that emphasize bird-in-the-hand teaching methods.

There's a small classroom and a conference room. On display was one of the largest news scrapbooks I had ever perused. Most prominent among recent stories was Mrs. T's White House visit in May 1984, when President Reagan presented her with the President's Volunteer Action Award. The President and some VIPs present in turn got a lesson in how to flap like a bird! This event marked the peak of a series of awards from other sources heaped upon this incredible woman during almost four decades of herculean efforts to interpret the natural world and to preserve more of it in Marin County.

The non-profit education center was created in 1975 by Don and Joan Bekins to perpetuate and expand Mrs. T's philosophy through media projects, as well as to offer training to potential Terwilliger Nature Guides. Joan spearheaded the formation of the docent volunteer teaching group in 1970. There are more than one hundred active nature guides that take hands-on programs into Marin classrooms and lead field trips at a variety of habitats on lands controlled by National Audubon Society, Nature Conservancy, the city of Mill Valley, county, state, and national parks. Mrs. T's dream is to have a larger Terwilliger Interpretive Center to provide a permanent home for the work of the naturalists and to be a prototype for others throughout the country. Joan also publishes books and other study materials that supplement science curriculum, including *Sights and Sounds of the Seasons*. More than one hundred pen and ink illustrations accompany a treasury of information written in Mrs. T's chatty style.

Tripping with Terwilliger may also be enjoyed at home or in the classroom by means of the five films (also available in video cassettes) that feature her in different habitats. They are available to schools on a free loan basis by writing Modern Talking Pictures, 5000 Park Street, North St. Petersburg, FL 33709.

Mrs. T has found time to work for several projects designed to preserve more open space for Marinites as well as for their flora and fauna. These range from bicycle paths to a monarch butterfly preserve to acquisition of Richardson Bay Wildlife Sanctuary for Audubon. Meanwhile the welcome workload of nature and conservation teaching reaches some 90,000 children each year! Nearly one million more in other counties and states are reached through her films each year.

We wonder what other ambitious project or goal Mrs. T at age seventy-seven will next reveal. We do know, at least, that she will never be content to rest on her laurels. Elizabeth Terwilliger is indeed "something special."

Tripping with Elizabeth Terwilliger (Elizabeth Terwilliger Nature Education Foundation photo).

Index

Abbott, Clinton, 17
Academy of Science, 73, 103
Adamson, Harry C., 38
Alameda Conservation Association, 84
Albright Training Center, 130
Aldrich, Elmer, 68
American Institute of Park Executives, 56
American Museum of Natural History, 87
Angel, Dick, 63, 124, 126
Anza-Borrego State Park, 12
Ardenwood Farm, 122
Arizona-Sonora Desert Museum, 131
Asilomar: 119; Conference Center, 68
Association of Bay Area Governments (ABAG), 99
Audubon: Association of the Pacific, 74; Camp of California, 106, 122; Camp of the West, 97; Canyon Ranch, 91; Golden Gate, 78, 96, 128; Hog Island Camp, 75; Marin, 93; National, 75, 87, 93, 96, 148; San Diego Society, 22; Sequoia, 93; Silverwood Sanctuary, 22; Wildlife Lecturer, 96
Audubon Canyon Ranch, 93
Austin, Rebecca, 47
Bacagalupi, Rimo, 111, 113
Baker, John, 96
Balboa Park, 7, 8
Barkin, Joshua, 62, 118–132
Barro Colorado, 78
Bay Farm Island, 72, 102
Behr, Peter, 84
Bekins, Don and Joan, 148
Bemiss, Homer, 27
Between the Devil and the Deep Blue Bay, by Harold Gilliam, 102
Big Boulder Ranch, 20
Blair Valley, 9
Blackburn, Robert, 70
Box Canyon, 3, 5, 9, 10
Brown, Kate, 6
Bryant, Harold, 74
Bug House, 27,28
Burress, Rex, 146

Butterfield Stage, 3
Butterfly Valley, 45
Cain, Brighton C., 26–38
California Department of Parks and Recreation, 130
California Gold Rush Centennial, 55
California Mammals, by Frank Stephens, 6, 11
California Native Plant Society, 65
California State Beaches and Parks, 66, 67
California State Parks Foundation, 70
Camp Dimond O, 33, 37
Camp Ohlone, 65
Chaney, Doreta W., 65
Children's Fairyland, 55, 56
Christmas Bird Count, 130
Civilian Conservation Corps (CCC), 123, 124
Cogswell, Howard, 139
Cooper Ornithological Society, 51, 74, 140
Coville, Frederick, 5
Coyote Hills Regional Park, 66, 128
Crab Cove Visitor's Center, 65
Crown Beach, 65
Darlingtonia californica, 45
Death Valley: National Monument 5, 43; Survey, 5
Del Norte County Historical Museum, 114
Dimond, Mike, 27n
Dimond Camp, 27, 33, 37
Ditmars, Raymond, 29
Drosera californica, 47
Drury, Newton, 68
East Bay Regional Park District, 61, 65, 83, 119, 122
East Bay Regional Parks, 27, 54, 63, 67, 120, 124
East Bay Veterinary Medical Association, 71
Eastwood, Alice, 74
Ehman, E. W., 53
Elsie Roemer Bird Sanctuary, 65, 84
Engle, Clair, 94
Environmental Protection Agency, 102

Erskin, Mrs. Morse, 100
Everett, Russell, 55
Farallon Island, 139, 140
Fenn, W. J., 6
Fish and Wildlife Service, 139, 140
Flora of Del Norte County, 110
Friends of the *Alma*, 125
Friends of the Botanic Garden, 64
Fun With Birds (film), 87
Gander, Mary, 16, 17, 20, 22
Gander, Frank F., 13–25
Gibsonville, Calif., 39, 40
Gilliam, Harold, 72, 85, 94, 100, 102
Golden Gate National Recreation Area, 146
Golden Gate Park, 79, 85
Grimwood, George, 53
Guillemot Cove, 103
Gulick, Esther, 100
Harbison, Charles, 17
Harter, Sam, 10, 12, 17, 24
Harwell, Bert, 96
Higgins, Mrs., 19
Hog Island, Maine, 75
Hornbeck, Hulet, 66
Huey, Laurence, 17
Indian Foods Cookout, 30
International Committee for Bird Preservation, 78
International Ornithological Congress, 76
Island in Time (film), 94, 95
It Began With a Roar, 7
Jepson, Willis Linn, 110, 111, 114
Jewel Lake, 124, 127
Joaquin Miller Park, 27, 53, 60, 61
Kahn's Alley, 58
Keddie Resort, 45
Kelly, Junea W., 72–85
Kerr, Kay, 100
Kissing Rock Garden, 19, 20
Knowland, Joseph R., 60
Knowland: Park, 59; State Arboretum and Park, 60; Zoo, 70, 71
La Porte, Calif., 35, 41, 47
La Puerte, 3, 8–11
Lake Merritt: 52, 53, 76; Breakfast Club, 34, 35; Waterfowl Refuge, 54, 91, 95
Lakeside Garden Center, 58
Lakeside Park, 30, 38, 53–55
Las Trampas Regional Park, 65
Lewton, David, 127

Limantour Spit, 93
"Living Sands of San Francisco Bay," 101
Los Mochos Camp, 37
Luckman, Irwin, 63
Magic Basket, The (film), 103, 105
Maidu Indians, 40, 41
Manual of California Flowering Plants, by Willis Jepson, 110
McCartney Marsh, 72, 84, 85
McLaughlin, Sylvia, 100
Merritt Community College, 11
Mewaldt, J. Richard, 138
Mexico's California (film), 97
Miller, Clem, 94
Miller, Juanita, 49
Morgan, Neil, 7
Mott, William Penn Jr., 38, 52–71, 95, 100, 124, 125, 127, 130
Mountain Beaver, 113
Museum of Vertebrate Zoology, 6
National Academy of Sciences, 74
National Park Service, 53, 54, 71, 74, 94, 130
National Wildlife Refuge, 129
Natural History Society, 7
Nature Conservancy, 148
Nature Puppet Theater, 126
Navelet, Arthur, 55
Nelson, Christian, 62, 124, 127, 131
New World Rediscovered (film), 97
Oakland, Calif.: 41, 45, 49; Airport, 84; All-City Youth Orchestra, 121; Park Commission, 61; Park Department, 61; Public Schools, 62
Oakland Ornithological Club, 30
Oakland Rotary Club, 38
Oakland Tribune, 60
Ohlone Indians, 31, 66, 81, 129
Old Lighthouse, 115
Old Sacramento Railroad Museum, 68
Old Town (Sacramento), 68
Ormondroyd, Edward, 122
O'Rourke Zoological Institute, 17
Pacific Flyway, 81, 139
Panama Pacific International Exposition, 6, 8
Park Naturalist, 30, 54, 55
Parker, Jack, 22
Parkinson, Ariel Reynolds, 90, 96, 99, 102, 103, 105
Parrott, Joel, 71
Peetz, John, 61

Peterson, Roger Tory, 90, 104
Pinnacles National Monument, 35
Point Reyes: Bird Observatory (PRBO), 138–140, 142; National Seashore, 138
Poison Oak, 59
Public Works Administration (PWA), 19, 53
Quincy, Calif., 45
Rabbit Creek, 39, 40
Ralph, John, 138
Rattlesnake, 29, 33–35
Raymenton, Dr., 17
Reading, John, 70
Reagan, Ronald, 66, 71, 148
Redwood National Park, 115, 116
Reynolds, Eric, 86–90, 93, 95–99, 101, 103, 104
Reynolds, Gordon, 90, 103
Reynolds, Laurel, 38, 81, 86–105
Rinehart, Amy, 39–51
Rinehart, Dr. Mike, 39–41
Ringtailed Cat, 21
Roberts, Ruth, 115
Roemer, Elsie, 73
Rotary Natural Science Center, 38, 57, 95
Rowantree, Lester, 108
Ruby Van Deventer County Park, 116
Russo, Ron, 129
Ruth, Ferd, 107
San Diego Museum of Natural History, 8, 17
San Diego Naval Hospital, 19
San Diego Society of Natural History, 7
San Diego Zoo, 7, 14, 16
San Diego Zoological Society, 7
San Francisco Bay, 63, 81, 91
San Francisco Bay (film), 102
San Francisco Bay Conservation and Development Commission (BCDC), 99, 102
San Leandro Bay, 81
San Ignacio Lagoon, 97
Save the Redwoods, 68, 109
Save San Francisco Bay Association, 100
Schultz, Ray, 33
Scripps, Ellen Browning, 8, 19
Sewellel, 113
Silverwood Audubon Sanctuary, 22, 24

Six Trips Afield, 74, 85
Sproul, Robert Gordon, 65
Smith River, 108, 109, 113
State Lands Commission, 84
State Parks Commission, 60
Stebbins, Robert C.,
Stephen T. Mather Training Center, 130
Stephens, Frank, 1–12
Stoner, Emerson A., 133–142
Strybing Arboretum, 85
Sunol Regional Wilderness, 12, 65
Talbot, Frederick C., 60
Terwilliger, Elizabeth C., 143–149
Terwilliger: Interpretive Center, 148; Nature Guides, 148
Thoman, Ronald C., 130
Tilden: Botanical Garden, 64; Environmental Center, 63; Nature Area, 62, 63, 123, 124, 126–129; Park, 64, 123, 125
Tilden, Freeman, 120
Torrey, Lehi, 72, 73, 84
Trudeau, Richard (Dick), 63, 65, 120
U.S. Army Corps of Engineers, 84, 99
U.S. Biological Survey, 2, 5, 135
U.S. Forest Service, 130
Udall, Stewart, 84
University of California: 6; Herbarium, 111
Use It, Use It Up (film), 102
VanBlocker, Jack, 10, 12, 17, 24
Van Deventer, Arthur, 109–117
Van Deventer, Ruby S., 106–117
Veirs, Stephen D., Jr., 117
Verlee, Jay, 70
Wegeforth, Harry M., 7
Western Bird Banding Association, 137
Western Discovery (film), 95
Western Foundation of Vertebrate Zoology, 142
Wild Animal Park, 7
William Penn Mott, Jr., Training Center, 68
Willis, Mindy, 97, 99, 101
Willis, Neal, 97–99
Witch Creek, 5, 6
Woodminster Theater, 53, 55, 61
Works Progress Administration (WPA), 19, 53
World Geological Congress, 74
Yucca Night Lizard, 35

BOOK DESIGN BY DAVE COMSTOCK.
COMPOSITION BY COMSTOCK BONANZA PRESS
AND DWAN TYPOGRAPHY.
SET IN HERMAN ZAPF'S PALATINO,
A TWENTIETH CENTURY TYPEFACE DERIVED
FROM CLASSIC ROMAN LETTER SHAPES.
PRINTED AND BOUND BY THOMSON-SHORE.